Space Time and Life 2

시 공 여 인 생　時 空 輿 人 生

글로벌콘텐츠
Global Contents

Space Time and Life 2
Written by Kim, Jeong-Il Ph.D
Published by Global Contents Publishing Group
(134-010 401, jungil BD 349-6 Gil-dong, Gangding-Gu, Seoul, Korea)

Space Time and Life 2
시공여인생 2

© 김정일, 2012

1판 1쇄 인쇄: 2012년 02월 25일
1판 1쇄 발행: 2012년 03월 05일

지은이: 김 정 일
펴낸이: 홍 정 표
펴낸곳: 글로벌콘텐츠
등 록_제25100-2008-24호

공급처: (주)글로벌콘텐츠출판그룹
이 사_양정섭
디자인_김미미
기획·마케팅_노경민·배정일·배소정
경영지원_최정임
주 소_서울특별시 강동구 길동 349-6 정일빌딩 401호
전 화_02-488-3280
팩 스_02-488-3281
홈페이지_http://www.gcbook.co.kr
이메일_edit@gcbook.co.kr

값 12,000원
ISBN 978-89-93908-38-1 93100

Space Time and Life 2

시공여인생

時空與人生

Preface

It was one moving work for myself. The initiation was from my father Kim, Choong Yeol. He was also a father of eastern philosophy in east Asia, and he still is. 43 years ago, he wrote his first book in Chinese: *時空與人生(Space Time and Life).* He made his little boy, five-year-old Kim, Jeong Il, do the book cover job in calligraphy. *Space Time and Life* is mainly about Chinese epistemology and metaphysics. Now, here in *Space Time and Life* 2, that little boy, deals with comparative philosophy and pragmatism on the table of cognitive science, all together, 'spatially'. He calls this forum: "spatial-philosophy".

This book is about closedness of causality and plasticity of the reality. I will discuss about epistemology of Chinese philosophy and American pragmatism against traditional western philosophy. I will run an unfavorable check on western method with Chinese and pragmatistic epistemology(of Peirce and Dewey). The squad of discussion will be cognitive science.

I will show that the obstacle of the West is due to its own epistemic foundation which lies on ontology and metaphysics. Thus, I will propose a new appreciation on the Chinese epistemic attitude and pragmatistic epistemology.

As the Bible says, the God made Adam out of mud. Up to the very moment that the God infused the mud sculpture with life, it was of the one muddy earth. But from the point the sculpture was given life as a human, an idea of 'I' came out, From then on, a dichotomy started taking a place between Adam and the world. Adam's 'I' was against all others of the one earth and must have been seen lonely to the God. Thus, the God made his pair, Eve, out of Adam. And again, until Eve was given life from the God, Adam/Eve was one. And as life was given, Eve, too, became her own 'I' against the world and against Adam. The relation between Adam and Eve from then on became 'one-to-one' situation.

Platonic Dualism of form and matter along with the Christian method of perception provided the footage of western epistemology. This was the beginning of the sequential epistemological dichotomy; 'I' or the 'world', 'I' or other 'I's, 'I' of mind or the rest of 'I' of body, ideal or corporeal, contingency or necessity and so on. We have seen all too many these 'a or b' business where we treat things in a dualistic scheme in which we habitually choose one 'superior or prior' or the other 'inferior or posterior'. But this kind of treatment could be, in fact, loosing the half of the whole or loosing it all. Why could we not take things in the form of 'a and b' in the 'whole' all together in harmony? This is the idea of *I Ching*; 'comprehensive harmony'.

The academic format of the West has been in the form of 'I vs the world': *'I', the 'knower' vs the 'world', 'to be known'*. The 'world', in traditional and still prevailing Lockian view, is the object that is to be represented in the knowers mind, and it may not be truly identical to the actuality. And in Humean view, the external world gives cause for a perception, but in the process of perception, the perceivers do not cause anything to the perceived objects. Perception is an 'one-way-relation' of causal dichotomy. And, this is the dichotomy that seems to provide the ground for almost all academic endeavors in the West. The 'world' and 'I' are in 'one-to-one' relation of dichotomy. We do philosophy taking the 'world': object, inquiring spatio-temporal causal antecedent to afford necessity. And this format of the causality has been good for the most but not for all. Thus, I will try to argue that this is the origin of epistemological hold especially for cognitive science.

The main points I wish to make in this book is that the world is not 'I's object. Instead of 'I vs the world', I will try to argue, in accordance to Chinese and pragmatistic epistemology, it is the case that 'I in the world'. 'Space and time' is the whole vessel of world. Thus, 'I' or any other beings exist in the scheme of 'space and time'. But in western philosophy, instead of 'life in general', we have the legacy of 'I' as 'knower' and mind as subject of knowing apart from the world. Unlike this traditional and conventional western philosophy, early proprietors of pragmatism have epistemological view that interestingly shares common ground with old China men's view of 'I' in 'space and time'. The crucial point is that 'I' is of 'my life'. Therefore, I propose to revaluate this concept of 'I' that is layed out in relation with "space, time and life".

This is book for my mentor, Kim, Yong Jeong.

CONTENTS

Chapter 1. Entering

This book is about closedness of causality and plasticity of the reality. It is about epistemology and metaphysics of traditional western philosophy, and Chinese philosophy and pragmatism on the contrast. In most cases, western philosophy understands Chinese philosophy with its own standard. On the contrary, in this book, I will criticize western method with Chinese and pragmatistic epistemology(focusing on Peirce and Dewey). The immediate perimeter of the discussion will be philosophy of mind or rather cognitive science. My goal is not to run a test for the accomplishment of the discipline, but to point out problems of causality and deterministic treat of mind. One of the problems, I argue, is due to the epistemic foundation which, after all, lies on ontology and metaphysics. Thus the discussion will move on to metaphysics. And finally, I will propose a new appreciation on the general Chinese epistemic attitude and pragmatistic epistemology and metaphysics.

The academic format of the West has been in the form of

'I vs the world': *'I', the 'knower' vs the 'world', 'to be known'*. The 'world', in traditional and still prevailing Lockian view, is the object that is to be represented in the knowers mind and it may not be identical to the actuality. And in Humean view, the external world gives cause for a perception, but in the process of perception, the perceiver do not cause anything to the perceived object. This is an 'one-way-relation' of causal dichotomy. And this is a dichotomy that seems to provide ground for almost all academic endeavors in the West. The 'world' and 'I' are in 'one-to-one' relation of dichotomy. We do philosophy taking the 'world': object, inquiring spatio-temporal causal antecedent to afford necessity. And this format of the causality has been good for the most but not for all. Thus, I will try to argue that this is the origin of epistemological problem especially for philosophy of mind and cognitive science.

One of the main points I wish to make is that the world is not 'I's object. Instead of 'the world or I' I will try to argue, in accordance to Chinese and pragmatistic epistemology, it is the case that 'I in the world'. 'Space and time' is unlimited, but 'I' exist within limited 'space and time': the world. Thus 'I' or any other beings exist in 'space and time': the one whole vessel. Unlike traditional and conventional western philosophy, early proprietors of pragmatism have metaphysical view that interestingly shares common ground with old China men's view of 'I' in 'space and time'. And their view of mind is layed out in relation with 'space, time and life'. But in western philosophy, instead of 'life in general', we have the legacy of 'I' as 'knower' and mind as subject of knowing.

As the Bible says, the God made Adam out of mud. Up to the very moment that the God infused the mud sculpture with life, it was the earth itself as one, and from the point the sculpture was given a life as a human, an idea of 'I' came out, then a dichotomy started taking places against the world. Adam's 'I' was against all others in the world and must have been seen lonely to the God. Thus the God made his pair, Eve, out of himself. And again, until Eve was given a life from the God, she and Adam were one. And as life was given, Eve became her own 'I' against the world and against Adam. Platonic Dualism of form and matter along with the Christian method of perception from the myth provide the philosophical arena of the West: epistemological dichotomy and metaphysical dualism; 'I' or the 'world', 'I' or other 'I's, I(as mind) or the rest of I(as body), rationality or the rest of mind, ideal or corporeal, contingent or necessary and so on. We have seen all too many these 'a or b' business where we treat things in a dualistic scheme and choose one as superior or prior and the other as inferior or posterior, so that, at the terminal, end up with dead-end dilemmas. The idea of choosing one out of two and make them line up in causal hierarchy is not acceptable in entire cases, but it could be ,in fact, loosing the half of the whole or loosing it all. Why can we not take things in the form of 'a' and 'b' and the 'whole' at once all together in harmony? This is the idea of the *I Ching*; comprehensive harmony. Of course this seems rationally unsound to the western standard for causality and time factor. '*li*' and '*chi*' concept is even worse, so that, a new term such as 'semi-dualism' was employed by Kim, Sang Il.

At this junction, I present different perspectives about Chinese philosophy and pragmatism concerning philosophy of mind and the metaphysics that underlies. A different look may give us a cracking point to make it out from the holding matters. It is certain that some mental states have causation but it seems not all there is to explain mental states. The current issues of digitalism in cognitive science especially around A.I. arena should be better off as a pure attempt of understanding mind-act or brain-act, not an attempt of theoretical simulating or actualizing mental state in any physical means. And I do address myself that the problem is on the foot of western epistemological attitude.

In chapter 2, philosophy of mind and cognitive science will be discussed. In this chapter, I will first lay out the hitherto passages of current address philosophy of mind. My strategy here would be to analyze chronological development of philosophy of mind and try to show, the various leagues of disciplines meet at the same obstacle: closedness of causality, fall short of plasticity, the limit of mechanistic explanation(in Peirce's term). I will present arguments against A.I. camp and refute the idea of "It's matter of time". I will try to show the various arguments including functionalism, connectionism, qualia and intentionality are all wedged in the matter of "plasticity"; namely biological feature of mind. I will go one step further in refuting 'thinking machine'. But, I will try not to fall into the technocratic turmoil of cognitive science. I will argue that any theory about mind solely on the line of causality principle is born refuted. It is not a matter of methodology. In chapter 2 section 3, I will derive the matter to epistemic and metaphysical scheme. The legitimacy of Newtonian physics, that rendered people to take natural laws as unchanging right answers of the universe, has long been withdrawn from the front line. Modern physics i.e., quantum physics and Prigogine's theory of the second law of thermodynamics suggests us the shape of universe that is not quite deterministic. What looks ordered is in fact in the self-organizing spontaneous changes from chaos(high entropy) to equilibrium. Nothing in this world is static nor purely individual, and the fluctuating changes are not predictable.

Pluralistic universe(Peirce's and James' term) i.e., dual aspects of light is another story. Photon and wave of light are not compatible in one system of physics. Peirce says that the universe is too vast to have a character. Due to these up-dated concepts upon universe, some front line natural science has already withdrawn from 'certainty' or singular solution for the universe. Western philosophy, in general, holds on to causality to rest on 'certainty'. Philosophy of mind and cognitive science which are on the extended line of analytic philosophy should look back and see where things started to go wrong. The answer appeals to the epistemic stance of the west: the principle of causality.

In chapter 3, Peirce's and Dewey's account of mind will be introduced. I will consider their theories are the major flow of pragmatistic view. They are quite remote from our current literature. For Peirce, every state of events in are organic form in this compound, complex process of the universe. Mind has no compartmentalized features of knowledge, will, feeling.

Rather, mind is compound of the three. Dewey, on the other hand, presents a biological; 'spatial and temporal' concept of mind. Peirce and Dewey both oppose physical reductionism. Dewey's account will be extensively discussed in order to drive the matter toward the common epistemological ground with Peirce's system. In section 3, Peirce's and Dewey's defense will be presented. Their theories are, in turn, attack on the traditional dualism. Peirce calls it "Cartesian Mistake" and Dewey calls it "Spectator theory." In this section, we can see how they can rest on their seemingly mystic theories on mind

In chapter 4, Chinese thoughts on mind in various writings will be discussed. It is not an easy task to make an affordable alinement between Chinese accounts of mind and that of the West. However, they are at least compatible with Peirce's and Dewey's accounts. Confucius' material hierarchy of development of mind will be presented. Hsün Tzu's and Chu Hsi's materialism and Huan T'an's theory of mental priority will be discussed. To discuss about mind and body problem, we ought to talk about '*li/chi*' concept, and in doing so, we ought to descend to '*t'ai-chi*' concept. According to Wen-Shan Huang's understanding of Chu Hsi, *li/chi* concept is dualism only for the sake of argument, but in real meaning, it is near-monism. And to be exact, it is not right to see the *li/chi* concept in western standard of dualism or monism. It seems that *li/chi* concept does not belong to either. *T'ai-chi*(Supreme Ultimate) concept may give us an idea to draw a line between the world of our immediate interests and the world beyond that. Same idea is argued by Peirce in his Metaphysical system. The goal of this chapter is to show how diverse Chinese philosophy of mind is from that of the west and. To see how Chinese philosophy and pragmatism rest on such theories of so-called 'mysticism'. We need to check on their epistemology and metaphysics.

Moving on to chapter 5, I will focus on epistemology and metaphysics. Of the various fields that Peirce worked on, this book will only deal with his theories coherent with the late-Peircian evolutionary cosmology. Of other philosophers such as James, Bergson, and late-Whitehead, I have chosen Peirce first, because he was the earliest one who brought out the idea of 'organismic universe' so it will not be wrong to take him as the initiator of the new doctrine in Anglo-American philosophy, and second, his cosmology of Tychism/Synechsm seemed appropriate to be compared with Lao Tzu's idea of dual aspect of '*Tao*', Thus, Peirce's system of truth will be brought out, and his view of organismic universe 'Tychism' and 'Synechism' will be compared with Man

-jan Cheng's understanding of Lao Tzu's '*Tao*' concept. I will try to construe them in a parallel line that Tychism and '*Ch'ang Tao*'(常道) in one side and Synechism and nameable '*Tao*' on the other. In discussing '*Tao*', P.T. Raju's comparative understanding of Confucian '*Tao*' and Taoists' '*Tao*' will be added. Dewey's anti-reductionism and anti-representationalism will be compared with James R. Ware's interpretation of Chuang Tzu's epistemology and cosmology: *liu-he-chih-nei*(六合之內) and *liu-he-chih-wai*(六合之外). I will call both attitude as epistemic monism. I will discuss common ground between Dewey's and Chuang Tzu's epistemology around the term "oneness". Thomé F. Fang calls this "comprehensive harmony". My discussion will be directed to a point that there are great similarities between Dewey's and Chuang Tzu's epistemological attitude.

In chapter 6, I will close the argument organizing the clusters of discussions. Western philosophy has been trying to solve its problems only within inbound methodology. Chinese philosophy or a side-streamer's view such as pragmatism were taken insignificantly by western philosophy in solving matters. Here, I propose to look onto the vintages of the west and the east as a methodological breaking out. It might be worth that the philosophy of mind that is doomed in the institutionalized causality-based approach would look for a new paradigm. A paradigm with different epistemic and metaphysical scheme might help us to move out from the difficulty of understanding mind's 'extra-causal and plastic character': the real feature of mental state.

Chapter 2. Philosophy of Mind and Cognitive Science

Until the recent time, mind/body problem has been dealt within the boundary of metaphysics. Theories about mind, as we see them today, were rather private stories based on hypothetical conjectures, conjectures that withstood all empirical questions. These stories can be sorted in three headings: Dualism, Material Monism, and Mentalism.

According to Descartes, 'mind' is the very first unit of certainty. 'Myself' is identified by my mind(thought). Mind as a unit is a conceptual boundary against the world. From my mind, the agent of my thought, rises the awareness of the world, thus thinking is the first ontological evidence for "I". Unfortunately, to this "mind", from which "I" as a being departs, about which Descartes was so certain that he starts his clear and distinct thinking for knowledge, *we do not have a direct access.*

And again, unfortunately up to this modern time, we still do know so little about our mind, brain, neural fiber and whatever you may call it. In the field of cognitive science, there are roughly two groups. One wishes to simulate brain work through mechanistic means and the other keep pointing out the problems of material reduction of mind to other physical means. We are not quite sure which party is right, but one thing is clear that both sides are playing their games on the arena where language of matter is colloquial. At this time being, from around 1950s there seems to be a visible breaking out in this discipline of causality and determinism about the study of mind or brain initiated by Gilbert Ryle. The goal of this chapter is to show basic problems on such approaches on mind based on causality, and at the end, in section 3, I will try to show that it has been due to systemic ground, and thus I will argue to elevate the whole matter onto epistemology and metaphysics to take a look at the matter focusing on inbound and outbound systems of science in general. The whole issue is not about cognitive science alone, but about breaking down the boundary or crossing over of different systems. *Our concepts on mind differ by our attitude of taking the world after all.* Thus my discussion, from then on, will deal with the western analytic attitude or stance in doing science and philosophy; epistemology and metaphysics.

2-1. Traditional Philosophy on Mind

The Cartesian substance dualism takes both mind and body as entities, thus, it should be called an ontological dualism. The sharp distinction of mind/body enabled to save certainly from the fusion of metaphysics. Mind or soul on one hand and body and other material things on the other. The material world including body is to be understood in mechanistic scheme, so that, the Cartesian methodology promoted the rapid growth of natural science that constructively cumulates clear and distinct empirical data of the material world as objective certainty. But, the uncertain side of the dualism, the ideal or immaterial side remains as mystery. So, as a whole set, Cartesian dualism, which claims that the world of what we know is referred by mind, and the ultimate features of mind can only be referred by the God, is a notorious confusion. In the Cartesian dualism, after all, there can not be an intelligible story to bridge immaterial mind to material body.

Monism as such Hobbes' takes mind as part of nature as epiphenomena. Hobbes' account that takes physical as 'real' gives some expedient treatment of human behavior toward desire, yet reserved mind in even more mysterious place. Hobbes' monism is explained by John Heil as follows:

> Materialism has a long history. Democritus(460-370 BC) described the world as a fleeting arrangement of atoms swirling in the void. Hobbes(1588-1679) and La Mettrie(1707-51) regarded mental phenomena as nothing more than mechanical interactions of material components.[1]

At this point the interaction between mental phenomena and the external world remains as unsolved. In this direction scientists take over matter and mind as relation between neurological brain act and mental phenomena. Hobbes' material monism can be considered to be one of the initiation for modern approach of mechanistic monism. John Heil goes on saying:

> …The more we learn about the nervous system, however, the more we discover apparent correlations between mental occurrences and neurological goings-on in the brain.(I follow custom and speak of goings-on in the brain.) This should, however, be understood as shorthand for goings-on in the central nervous system. Alternatively, we could think of the brain as distributed throughout the body.[2]

---

1) John Heil, *Philosophy of Mind*, Routledge, 1998, p. 53.

2) Ibid., p. 71.

Heil takes mind reduced to some biological phenomena. Berkeliean idealistic mentalism is a bit 'mental' to start with. However, His idealism which takes the world some kind of fantasy or unreal is hardly intelligible. Strawson explains Berkeliean idealism as follows:

> Berkeley is not a strict idealist, because he does not hold that ideas or experience are all that exist. He also holds that minds exist, and he rejects the strict idealist bundle or stream or pure process theory of mind, according to which minds are entirely constituted out of ideas.[3)]

According to what Strawson says above, Berkeley rather gives weight on inner mind events, but, his view should not, in a strict sense, called a pure mentalism. Even though Strawson is right about Berkeliean idealism, the problem of the relation between mind and external objects remains. So far in this section, three traditional accounts on mind were discussed; dualism, monism and mentalism. All these three traditional kinds treat mind as a mysterious entity.

---

3) Galen Strawson, *Mental Reality*, The MIT Press, 1994, p. 112.

2-2. Problems in Cognitive Science

- Footing -

With the growth and advance of natural science, the developments render many useful facts about the character of mind and thus the problem of mind descended from metaphysics down to science. Scientists' reports on brain now provide great implication to contemporary cognitive science. There are various contemporary literature concerning brain activity. Mainly, their goal is to build mechanistic models that simulate our brain work. The attempt is somehow focused, at the end, on the method of how precisely interpret the analogous world into digital sign operation. And, some scientists believe that it is a matter of time. People started to take the matter more actively.

The materialists[4)] such as Ryle, Smart, Lewis, Armstrong, Shoemaker, and etc... understand our mind of psyche in cause and effect relation in between input and output, and it is genuinely reducible to physico-chemical events. The material substances that make up minds are the same that make up rocks

---

4) The terms can be varied: behaviorism, physical monism, reductionism, identity theory.

and trees. If the particles are arranged in the right way, the material will have mind. It is generally a reductionist's theory. In this view, the terms 'brain' and 'mind' are taken identically(Type-Type Identity Theory). Its method is to study behaviors to understand related mental event. Of course, there is non-reducible materialism such as Donald Davidson's 'anomalous monism'. But, it is also clear that Davidson's monism is based on at least some causal interaction between mental events and physical events. It can not escape from being in a dualistic form of mind and matter relation. The major criticism on material monism carried out by Putnam basically overlaps with his criticism on functionalism discussed below. This first generation philosophy of mind(as we may call) failed because they were lack of empirical data or technological back-up, and mostly, they treated mind and mental events related to and reduced to physical cause and effect under strict deterministic laws.

In 1949, Gilbert Ryle's *The Concept of Mind*[5)] put an end of the era where philosophy of mind was taken as metaphysical problem. The concept of mechanized-information-process was a result of the development of digital computer technology. A

5) Gilbert Ryle, "Introduction," *The Concept of Mind*, Hutchinson & Company, Ltd., 1949.

tempting project out of this technology is that we can explain our brain act with the mechanistic theory and, furthermore, in principle, we can build a computer that works identical with our brain. Therefore, the goal for cognitive science become to find the best model to proceed. The traditional behaviorism understands our mind of psyche in cause and effect relation in between input and output, so that, this genuinely material principle reduces mind to a physico-chemical events. Theorists announced that problem of mind would be dealt in the field of science and the new label was cognitive science.[6] From then on, that most popular issue in cognitive science was functionalism.

- Functionalism and Multiple Realization -

Functionalism, as first introduced by Putnam[7] was to revive

---

6) On this context Dennet called the traditional philosophy up to the point of cognitive science an arm-chair philosophy.

7) The functionalist approach was first introduced by Putnam's "Psychological Predicates", *Art Philosophy and Religion*, University of Pittsburgh Press, 1967. His original intention with the functionalism was to against the traditional materialism such as Smart's. But, the idea of 'multiple realization' gave a fresh reinforcement to the A.I. researchers whose goal is to realize brain act in materialistic way. Because of this Putnam became a critic of functionalism, his own invention. Critics comment on his changes in position, but Putnam defences himself in many of his writings, that machine brain was not his idea, in fact, his

the separation of mind from physico-chemical matter. But unlike the original intention of Putnam, the major feature of functionalism, the "multiple realization", spurred the possibility of thinking machine. Functionalism accepts mind as entity, non-material but in the material residence of brain within cause and effect chain. This idea that mind exists on top of material brain seems a total fiction for naive materialists. In a strict sense, there hides a character of dualism beneath the surface: immaterial property of a function and purely physical means of realization. What functionalism suggests is that mind is a function within material phenomena and, yet, it is irreducible to matter(Fodor and Harmaan are also on this line).

For realization of a certain function, infinite number of means are possible; "multiple realization". Regardless of material or design, when a machine works as certain function, the function can not be reduced to constituting matters. A machine can be built with different material in different design to perform exactly same function as the former. Functionalism(computational) sees our brain similarly: regardless of hardware or wetware, works as computer, in principle. The idea is that the function called "mind" can be realized by both brain and computer. This implies that human

---

idea is quite the opposite.

mental state is not restricted to be a biological system. Functionalism, thus forecasts the coming of mechanical brain. The rule-based computational model was widely discussed for the idea of machine brain. A function is itself a process between input and output. An identical state may be shared by stuffs with different physical makeup. And crucially, algorithm that any rule-based model must have is characteristic operation of cause and effect which is the principle rule of materialism.

- Chinese Room Argument -

For the A.I.[8] advocates, as the suggestion that mechanized - information - processing is possible as the Turning machine test has shown, the coming of computer functioning just like a human brain seems only a matter of time. For this point Searle and Putnam give important arguments. In "Chinese Room Argument", Searle attacks the A. I. claiming that computer and brain can not possibly share same mental state[9]. Searle's argument is in short as follows.

A man who does not know chinese language is in a room

8) abbreviation of 'Artificial Intelligence'.

9) John Searle, "Minds, Brains, and Programs," *Behavioral and Brain Sciences*, vol.3, 1980, pp. 417 ~ 457.

where only chinese language can be used. The idea to process data is that he has a certain device that translates Chinese into English. Thus following the instruction of the device he successfully perform data written in Chinese. In this case, can we say that the man know Chinese language? Searle's point here is that what the man does is just following instruction to do the job and it is not the same as when a Chinese language user does the same thing.

What the man actually perform is not Chinese but English. In the same token what computers do are not the same as the brain acts, even though a computer performs a same level of activity, what the computer feels and understands in the course of the act is different from that of a human when he or she produces same performance. But Searle's argument is not so strong for a reason that it is not quite clear how we see that different processes with an identical result can be seen differently. Searle's main point seems to oppose the possibility of 'semantical' ascend of 'syntax' and this implies the impossibility of multiple realization of brain directly.

- Putnam's Argument on Functionalism -

For the same matter, Putnam presents two arguments[10),

Holism Argument and 'Gödelian Argument'. In holism argument, Putnam claims that for a computer to act as a human does, it must be programmed with algorithm that includes generally human intelligence, reason, and the whole capacity of understanding. The algorithm has to have every reasoning related to every possible humanly action. This algorithm is impossible. Furthermore, in Gödelian argument, Putnam claims that even such a algorithm is possible, we can not, in principle, know if it is right. No matter how ingenious and perfect the algorithm may get, in principle, it is always possible to be falsified. This is from the Gödelian argument that for whatever reason can formalize, reason can go beyond. Putnam's idea is that it is impossible, in principle, to make out a total set of algorithm representing our mental act.

Computational rule-based model is blocked by its own principle not by current technical deficiency. Putnam employs Wittgenstein's theory of family resemblance to reinforce his holism argument against functionalism. Two apparently identical functions are in fact sharing some common ground. When it comes to concept of meaning, a whole meaning of a event or a state is unique only by itself. A meaning can not

---

10) Hillary Putnam, "Mind Language and Reality," *Philosophical Paper*, Vol II, Cambridge, 1975.

be fulfilled by other meanings. Considering a function, things are more complicated. A simple fact is that we can not give a "full name" upon a single function. We can only give a name for 'a priori' event or state. A name may fully bind in denotative sense. For 'a posteriori' event or state ,in connotative sense, we can not give a "full name". This way of understanding names might give a help to accomplish the main goal of Putnam's holism argument.

Here, I will go one step further in refuting functionalism. Suppose we fully acquired a name and algorithm for a function, then such algorism should be able to alter itself constantly for the constant changes of the environing circumstances. We all know for sure that external conditions and their relation to a subjective mind ever changes, and most of all, biological mind is not static. Can we come out with such self-changing and self-adjusting algorithm? It does not seem possible in deterministic rule-based concept of computation. For a biological feature of mind, computational models fail.

- Problem of Qualia -

When it comes to computations, for the capacity which only requires syntactic processing, computers already far exceed human capacity. Some other things thinking computer can not explain are some peculiar character of mind such as qualia, and it eventually leads the matter to the problem of intentionality. Imagine two men sharing exactly identical brain function. Yet, it is possible that two men's mental state can be identical when they are exposed to different sense stimuli and the vice-versa,[11] i.e., different colors may function identically, then they clearly have different qualitative mental states.

'Absent qualia' is another argument of this sort. Pain will be a good example. Pain for one man could be joy for the other. When a human asks painkiller for a headache, an android which is designed to function same as a human may ask for a painkiller without an identical headache. Machine Functionalism can not explain this, because, the concept of function is the process between input and output whose algorithm must have mechanical operation of cause and effect. Intentionality is Brentano's term for mental character. It is 'aboutness' or 'directedness'[12]. In the physical level, when I see something, my eyes are directed to some object. When there

---

11) Block, Ned J. and Fodor, Jerry, "What Psychological State are not," *The Philosophical Review*, Vol 81, 1972, pp. 159~181.

12) Dennet, Daniel, "Intentional System," *The Journal of Philosophy*, Vol. 68, 1971, pp. 81~106.

is no matching object for my vision of it, it is just an illusion. It is in cause and effect relation: the sense stimuli, the cause, and the vision on my retina, the effect. The mechanical rule between object and its image can not be broken; no object, no image. However, examples of intentionality such as 'hope', 'belief', and 'fear' are not about a definite objects to be matched. Like the case of qualia, this intentional character of brain can not be explained by cause and effect mechanism, because, 'Closedness' is a principal rule of cause and effect chain[13]. Searle's argument on semantic engine, Putnam's argument against multiple realization, qualia problem and intentionality all together toss our problem of thinking machine over to the compositional plasticity: namely extra-causal, biological feature.

- Connectionism -

If we retreat for a moment from making human level of thinking machine, a lower form of information processor is possible. And if the device can be acquired with learning capacity, the project is still valid. To have learning capacity

13) Kim, Jae-Gwon, *Philosophy of Mind*, West View Press, 1996, ch. 6, sec. 8.

is to have capacity of organismic growth. The special character of mind such as qualia and intentionality can only be acquired by flexibility between input/output mechanism, and this is to be called 'plasticity'[14] for the argument. And, plasticity is a character of organismic brain; namely - pattern recognition, active correction of distorted input, rehabilitative reaction for injured system, adaptation through generalizing the received(learned) knowledge···etc. To have this capacity, although it associates itself with material monism, it is necessary to break out from the material mechanism that prevents organismic change. An organismic change can only be explained, in materialists view, as a defect or fallacy of a system because cause and effect system has to be carried on in strict deterministic machinism where no popping of a new thing nor a room for a flexible operation is possible.

As a result of the continuous exploration of the cognitive science, the relation between brain activity and computer is repeatedly discussed. The functionalism attempted to explain brain activity by devising a model of cognition with the principle of computer, i.e., mechanistic-information- processing, algorithm,

14) The term "plasticity" is a borrowed term from aesthetics. It is an opposite term for what is 'fixed' or 'determined'. In aesthetics its meaning is ability to make new image or form or fashion. The term seems to be adequate to stand for what closed mechanism lacks.

digital operation, turing machine, etc. However, this kind of computational or rule-based approach is now taken to be inadequate in explaining the complex and peculiar nature of mental activity. Thus this kind of approach of artificial intelligence has already been discharged. But in the continuous pursuit for a better model resulted a presence of connectionism which in broad sense is another up dated version of functionalistic model. While the rule-based model has a linear structure, the connectionists' model has a parallel structure. Stephen Burwood explains the plausibility of connectionists' model. It's advantageous point is it's biological character of operation.

> Connectionists regard their proposal as more biologically plausible because the network they are using as models resemble the biological neural networks in the brain more closely than the language of thought model does.[15)]

The connectionists' model has a parallel distributed processing(P.D.P.) system with web structure. This P.D.P system seemed to break the limits that current digital computer models have-namely; pattern recognition, active correction of

15) Stephen Burwood, *Philosophy of Mind*, University of Hull, UCL. Press, 1998, p. 61.

distorted input, organism reading for injured system, adaptation for environment through generalizing the received(learned) knowledge. The organismic and analogous character of connectionists' model could provide a better explanation for our brain structure if it truly does what this theory claims it does.

Instead of giving a program to the central system, connectionist system learns to handle the input by the provided rules of learning. The system theoretically operates by nodes in the neural web with each activated level for an input; either to proceed forward or inhibit. The special character of the system is, unlike the traditional system that data are stored by address, the idea of storing data by content(content addressable memory). This ability enables the system to process data that are partial or distorted. The system has an organic feature such as learning ability.

But the design principles for connectionists' model are still questioned: How do we give it a right instruction? How does it store symbols for syntactic motor? and so on. Dreyfus gives an argument of initial learning instruction for generalization of learned data. Even a self-learning device must have an initiating pattern of learning which means the self-learning ability of a device is only possible by human design. There are various disciplines under the connectionists' camp. They are still under dispute. But the connectionists' model is on the same route with the computational system, for, they too try to realize mental cognition by functional simulation. Its operational principle lies on the method of mapping between input and output[16].

Dreyfus' argument of initiating of learning ability may not entirely refute the attempt to acquire biological feature of mind. Minds of lower life forms are functioning upon basic instincts which are in a way compared to a given initial pattern of learning. It will not be wrong that even a higher life form's mentality such as human beings are partially governed by natural instincts. However, I argue that as long as connectionism is a subclass of functionalism, it will not escape from the holism argument. Most of all, the initial endowment of pattern of learning from human inhibits the machine to be developed as an organismic thinking entity. The assumed process between input and output an activated node will connect the chain. If we draw a line on input-chosen activated node-output, in a strict sense, we see a closed causal chain. Because of this closedness of causality, connectionism also fails

---

16) Kim, Yeong Jung, 金泳楨, *Philosophy of Mind and Cognitive Science*, Philosophy and Current Matters Co., 1996, p. 189.

to fulfill plasticity of mind.

2-3. Some Problematic Arguments on Epistemic Stance: Closedness of Causality and Material Reductionism

Current address philosophy of mind or cognitive science has come to a point of pause where our exploration on mental state can go no further but stay. Theories including mind/body dualism and material monism are layed out under the strict deterministic laws, the laws that are based upon causality with which all other external phenomena of the nature have been explained. The main problem of causality in philosophy of mind is that it can not explain thc plastic nature of mind in the form of causal input-output relation.

I argue that researching mind with language of matter is only binding up-to certain level. It is like discussing principle of color with principle of sound or discussing principle of circle with principle of straight line. We should, first of all, accept that material and mental are two different things. Before that, of course we need to accept an attitude of the limit to understand the world with language of matter. Connectionism tried to achieve plastic character of organismic changes of mind, but it is shown that it too can not free itself from causal closedness. At this point, we may make an inquiry whether we are in a right position and right direction in discussing the matter. We do know that causal closedness or deterministic strictness are the major obstacle. Then, how did we come to this dead-end point of the discipline? I argue that it is due to our epistemic stance.

As Descartes says, 'I' or 'mind' is the first unit of certainty and knowing. 'I'-'the knower' take 'the world'-'the known' separately, so that, a dichotomy of 'I' against 'the world' is inevitable. Perhaps, this dichotomy of 'I' against 'the world' is a necessary basic format for any epistemology. Our perception about the world has to be obtained in our mind which is in-bound 'myself' against the out-bound world.

The boundary between our mind and the world is the very basic format of knowing. To have any knowledge, we must have mind that can house the knowledge. and also we need object of knowledge that is something apart from mind. There are two important points in knowing. One is that without experience objects can not be perceived. And second is that every experience is carried out within the domain of time, and any perceived object other than inner mental event exists in space. Thus, space-time and 'I' are the basic format of dichotomy of knowing. This format of dichotomy goes on. 'I' of my mind is separated from the rest of 'I' of my body. 'The world' of ideal is separated from the world of matters which are spatio-temporal, imperfect and less real.

In traditional Lockean epistemology, the objects in the world are obtained in mind as representation. The world itself and its representation in mind are not the same things. The initiation of the representation in mind is triggered by the external cause of the world objects. This is the starting point of causation in our perception of the world. Here, we should keep it in mind that the causation of perception process in western traditional view is always one-way relation which means only objects that perceived give causes for perception in mind. Mind's will or belief does not cause anything to external objects. This is how causality takes place in Western epistemology. Hume's account does an important role in this traditional epistemology. Colin Mcginn illustrates this as follows:

> …for the real, David Hume never denied the objective reality of causal necessity. He firmly believed in it. And so Hume's reputation is set to rise high again. He did not, after all, commit the mistake of letting in ideational contents of our minds determine what the world might really contain.[17)]

---

17) Colin Mcginn, *Mind and Bodies,* Oxford Univ. Press, 1997, p. 164.

The important point that Hume makes is that, for a certainty of our external perception, perceived objects must be guaranteed purely objective and unaffected by perceiver's mind. This means that if the perceivers mind moves around one can not perceive exact figure of the object. For better achievement of certainty in perceiving the objective world, we start dividing the objects into two, prior and posterior. We take a prior more certain. For certainty in perceiving the world object, we look for necessitating causal antecedence of events or a states. It is naturally believed that necessity can be provided by causal antecedence.

Then such causal antecedence requires prior causal antecedence for a firmer certainty; causal chain is to be. With the same manner, we look at objects into it's constituents. As we go obtaining smaller particles as constituents of certain events and states are satisfactorily secured by causal chains. Thus, the prior and the smaller are taken for certainty. This format of knowing is very fundamental in traditional Western epistemology and, in fact, it owes its origin to Democritus' Atomism.[18)]

18) In our ordinary language we ask questions with "Why" and answers usually start with "Because". As the word "because" is made up with two words "be" and "cause", we can see that any answer starts with "because" provides the cause of the problem itself. The question may not be settled until "Why" is run out. This is another example of causal

We hold on to causality as general rule of knowledge. This epistemology with causality on top of collected empirical data nourished the growth of natural science. And thus, as science consequently grew up, causality became more important in most academic disciplines. When we come to look back, we see that most of this epistemological stance is initiated from the dichotomy of 'the world' and 'I'.

In natural science, method of causality with empirical data is considered to provide natural laws. The natural laws that science provided were taken as eternal truth of the world. Newtonian physics has started this new period of laws of nature which took over the place of the Church. In this ever changing unstable world, scientists cumulated regularities in natural events and started to call them laws that never changes, eternal true stories of the universe.

Newton gave a new look on the world. In space and time, the basic format of any physical state of affair, Newton explained basic laws of physics in his theory of gravity, velocity and motion. And he proved his theories with common method of causality and mathematics. Here, the basic language of natural laws is causality. Up until the turn of the 20th century,

---

chain, a chain of "Why" and "Because". In most cases, as we wish, the question of "Why" may never rest. We notice here that in our process of knowing, the epistemic chain of causality entails.

along with Newtonian trend, causality was on its regime in study of this deterministic world.

We all know now that more findings in physics, however, opened a new era in science. Researches on subatomic level quantum physics has discovered the fact that it is not the case that things in this universe are in strict deterministic system.[19] In upward way, we see the universe in macro-vision that our solar system and galaxy and beyond that, the whole cosmos seems deterministic. However, downward way with micro vision, quantum physics has shown that in the subatomic world, there are protons and electrons that revolve around the protons just as the planets revolve around the sun. When we observe the atom of hydrogen with modern means of physics, we notice a negative electrons' dizzy circuits revolving around positive nucleus at the rate of six thousand billion times per second.

It is important that the fusion or irregularity of subatomic movement is not due to the lack of technology. It is just the way they are. Our developed faculty has gone down to the level of 'quark' at the moment and, in such a subatomic level, things are not deterministic. What seems to be deterministic before is now found fussy and irregular.

Ilya Prigogine gives us a new paradigm on the view of

19) http://www.jracademy.com/~jtucek/science/what.html.

fluctuating universe. What seems ordered and deterministic is in fact near-equilibrium in constant fluctuation. Prigogine placed on the second law of thermodynamics saying that physical system fluctuate spontaneously and irreversely toward disorder. This is called 'entropy'. If there is energy of lifting up of entropy, the universe will fall to a thermal death. High level of entropy means a chaos and disorder and lowest level of entropy means equilibrium and order. As simply stated above entropy is a system only for resulting thermal blow out. But the universe is consisted with other system, 'system of dissipative'. Each system compensates each other and outputs something look like 'self-organized'. The universe is systems ongoing fluctuation of nonequilibrium and equilibrium. Two thing we notice from Prigogine's law of entropy are first universe is not deterministically static and second, nothing in this universe is purely isolated[20].

In this new vision of the universe, traditional deterministic scheme of cause/effect is now taken limited in forming the vision of the world. This can be called organismic view of the universe. Peirce and Dewey's organismic view of the universe will be discussed along with the Chinese metaphysics below.

---

20) Kim, Yong Jeong, 金鎔貞, "Entropy and Prigogine's Dissipative Structure," *Science Philosophy and Culture*, Bum Yang Sa, 1996.

Kim, Yong Jeong writes about this as following:

> We believe we are going on to a new naturalism, This naturalism is in a direction of comprehension. Eventually we are going to combine quantifying, formalizing theoretic attitude of the west and spontaneous self-organizing system of eastern tradition. This is a wish for western traditional analytic method and eastern organistic and holistic method go together.[21]

This kind of attitude in physics has altered the epistemic stance in natural science, therefore, some modern science has withdrawn itself from certainty, so has our metaphysical scheme. It would not be wrong to say that the era of logical positivism is now over.

Another development in modern physics that falsifies the certainty of natural law is the concept of pluralistic features of the universe.[22] Peirce argues that what we accept as truth

---

21) Ibid., p. 169.

22) In the late 20th century, the main flow of Western philosophy was philosophy of the absolute. Peirce objected to this view that it is not possible to obtain a single system that accounts for various forms of the nature and life. James formalized this view in his term 'Pluralistic Universe' in "the type of philosophical thinking" in The Writings of William James. Dewey on the other hand, used the term `pluralistic knowledge or experience' in the sense of ever changing individuals and the environment or nature to which they attached. Dewey is opposed

in science may only be a part of factual affair of the world. Peirce says:

> Universe ought to be presumed too vast to have any character.……That all science rolls upon presumption(not of formal but of a real kind) is no argument with them, because they cannot imagine that there is anything solid in human knowledge.[23]

As shown above, Peirce takes science nothing but presumption(except for formal science) of the universe, so that the vastly characterized will not be wedged in a certain shape. Peirce takes current science as a set of coherent body that tries to appeal to the entire character of the universe, but the true story of the universe is yet to be explained.

Dual character of light is a good example for this.[24] Light has character of both wave and particle. Both characters of light have experimental bearings, so that, neither could be

---

to anything static in *Reconstruction of Philosophy*. Later this view of Pluralistic Universe became a motto of late Whitehead's philosophical view.

23) *Collected Papers of Charles Sanders Peirce*,(hereinafter CP) The Belknap Press of Harvard Univ. Press, 1965, Book 6, paragraph 421.

24) *McGraw-Hill Encyclopedia of Physics*, Sydil P. Paker & McGraw-Hill Inc. 1981, p. 679.

wrong. But at the same time, both can not be compatible at one set of scientific system. Should we ask if the coherent body of science of the time being is a total fiction? It is much more fruitful that we conclude that it might be the case that when our system of science comes up with a finding that is to be true nature of a state of affair, it can be just a partial character of that state of affair. Kim, Yong Jeong writes about this matter as following:

> We have a knowledge that the French physicist Louis de Broglie developed, a mathematical theory according to which each little particle of matter, too is accompanied by a wave. That is to say, the "either-or" was thus replace by an "and," and from de Broglie's discovery, therefore, dates the duality of interpretations, which ever since has been confirmed as an inescapable consequence or the nature of matter. The subatomic occurrence naturally was recognized as not being determined by a casual law...[25]

There are two things we need to notice from the above passage. First is that either 'a or b' concept of dichotomy is now no more fully binding mechanism in approaching to the

25) Kim, Yong Jeong, "The Dissolution of a Material Substance and the Description by Space or Field," *Philosophy and Science*, Bum Yang Sa, 1997, p. 487.

answers of the nature. And second deterministic mechanism is no more the sole principle in understanding the world. Thus, our current body of science is to deal with pluralistic and organic features of the universe. At this point, it seems wiser to drop our attempt for eternal, unchanging truth or right lexical concept of answers for the universe.

In this chapter, I discussed philosophy of mind and its problems. After that, I addressed main problems of scientific theories in two heading; quantum physics and pluralistic features of universe. My strategy here is to show the current matter of cognitive science in understanding and simulating brain act is based on causality and deterministic strictness. Mind is rather flexible, plastic and organismic in nature, and most of all, we do know so little about it.

Even some natural science has given up deterministic scheme. And it is now known that the universe is not in a shape of all and all hierarchy of causal chain. We should see the same in the field of cognitive science(both A.I. camp and anti-materialists), thus, philosophy of mind needs to be reshaped related to the law of causality. We have traced back to see the origin of causality problem which was after all our epistemic stance of taking the world in two-fold dichotomy. Dichotomy of subject and object and dichotomy of objects 'a or b'. As we have seen above, even current science does not exactly pursue to afford static 'a or b' kind of answer. Statistic or regularity may replace 'certainty' in natural science. We have noticed these movement from the changes of scientific epistemic stance such as 'verificationism', 'falsificationism', 'anarchism', and so on. Philosophy has to step down from ideology. Now, let us take a look at Peirce's and Dewey's pragmatistic version on the world and mind and Chinese thoughts on mind and metaphysics. They have been doing philosophy on the ground of indeterministic scheme. My aim is not to point out the diversity between the two, but to possibly match the common features of the two to strengthen the side-streamer of western philosophy.

Chapter 3. Peirce's and Dewey's Account of The World

Peirce and Dewey are both having scientific attitude upon nature and human mind under Darwinian evolutionary cosmology. They are quite apart from traditional western epistemology and metaphysics. They disavows the idea of Greek concept of 'soul'. Influence of Christianity in western philosophy seem to be intentionally filtered in Peirce's and Dewey's arguments. Peirce argues that matters about mind is a task of scientific investigation concerning nerve and stimuli system.

Dewey, on the other hand approaches on biological ground. Dewey explains that as a life form develops at a certain point, related locomotion in space and time, mentality emerges. Dewey calls his theory 'emergent theory.'[26] In both Peirce's and Dewey's system, there is trace of material reduction. However, we can not just call them material reductionists, because both

---

26) S. Alexander used the term "emergent theory of mind" in his book *Space, Time, and Deity*, Dover Publication Inc. New York, originally Published in 1920, Dewey calls his theory of mind "emergent theory" but the two are not likely related. Dewey's theory was so named in terms of biological concept and left out the concept of god or deity.

employ mystic emergence of psyche in due course of material development. Thus, our goal is first to look at their ideas on mind and second, most importantly, is to see how they, as scientists, can rest on mystical jump in natural phenomena.

As scientists Peirce and Dewey accept the nature of humanly understanding and the world that are beyond conventional scientific causal deterministic approach. What they argue is ,in a word, "organismic concept of the world." As we see their epistemology and metaphysics, we will find the basic common grounds with Chinese philosophy in general. Further discussion of Peirce's and Dewey's metaphysical ground will be included chapter 5 with Chinese metaphysics and epistemology.

3-1 Peirce's Organismic View of Mind

> Blest are those whose blood and judgment are so well commingled that they are not a pipe for fortune's finger to sound what stop she please. Give me that man that is not passion's slave, and I will wear him in my heart of hearts. *Hamlet*, chapter 3-2[27)]

Above passage from *Hamlet* tells us that passion and reason are not separated divisions of mind. It seems Shakespeare

27) Shakespeare, *Hamlet*, W. W. Norton & Company INC., 1963.

believed that ,in mind, different features are mingled as one. The traditional dualism takes mind separate from body, the division goes on to separate reason from rest of mind. Traditional view on mind is like the idea of an orchestra in which various instruments separately play and the outcome is commingled sound of a tune. Even in an orchestra, there is 'cadenzza'[28] where the tune is conducted by a solo instrument. The theme of *Hamlet* is thus a young man's struggling to be purely resonable in decision making. Shakespeare's point seems that it is absurd to single out reason from rest of mind. Peirce also thinks that mind is a compound of different features. The most important part in Peirce's theory of mind is the idea of 'compound'.

> Almost all the Philosophers of the century have agreed to name feeling, knowledge and will as the parts the mind, or to speak more accurately as the three classes of state of mind.(CP 6, 540)

---

28) In an orchestra, in a cadenzza section, only one instrument plays a tune and all other instruments behind it make no sound until they all join together to resume the continuing flow of the tune. When we see this in a holistic view, the waiting instruments that are making no sound are doing their part in making the tune of the one whole orchestral tune. This might be interpreted as a proper analogy of Lao Tzu's idea of being becomes non-being and non-being becomes being. This will be discussed in the chapter 5.

Peirce does not agree on this three classes of state of mind. Peirce argues that man has no compartmentalized departments(Peirce's term) of feeling, knowledge and will in mind. One's inner life and nature are rather a compound of the three and even instinct. The three departments of mind interpenetrate each other. No reason is possible alone without feeling and will, and no feeling or will is possible alone.[29] Our minds are compound of complex and peculiar process.(CP 6, 540–552)

As a producer of terminology Peirce uses his own term "Psychognosy" in explicating the nature of mind. Psychognosy can be taken by meaning in between 'psychical' and 'physical'. Peirce is material monist but has a theory different from that of mind/body identity theory. Peirce attains that ontological status of mind is on top of materialism.

However, upon the traditional concept of 'soul', Peirce does not attribute ontological status.

> I am not speaking of soul, the metaphysical substratum of mind(if it has any), but of mind phenomenally understood. To get such a conception of mind··· as the science of dynamics affords of matter, or material events, is a business which can only be accomplished by resolute

29) Here, Peirce used the term 'knowledge' and 'reason' interchangeably.

scientific investigation.(CP 6, 365)

It seems clear for Peirce that matters concerning mind are to be taken in the field of science. The traditional Christian and Greek concept of soul is that apart from the entire mind soul is uniquely differentiated to be immortal and is something over and above the rest of mind. This special concept of soul is nothing but a fiction to Peirce. According to Peirce, physiology and psychology tell us that mind's psychognosy is synthesis in process of neural stimuli. But unlike material monists or reductionists, Peirce gives psychical factor on the physical make up. Thus, Peirce is not a material reductionist. The physical character of mind is illustrated:

> It can never be explained, unless we admit that physical events are but degraded or undeveloped forms of psychical events.(CP 6, 263)

Peirce, then, distinguishes external and internal phenomena. No matter what the cause is, the event of experiencing includes inter participation and Peirce clearly differentiates inner event from external events which are physical. On one hand, Peirce accepts, the idea of physical make-up of mind, and on the other hand, Peirce holds on to mind as inner event which could be called purely mental.

> Experience being something forced upon us, belongs to the external type. Yet in so far as it is I or you who experience the constraint, the experience is mine or yours, and thus belongs to the inner world.(CP 6, 439)

It is clear that Peirce conceives mind as a scientist. Scientific investigation will find out more and more about mind. But unlike other monists, Peirce saves a room for purely psychical events, a room apart from general physical events. For this reason Peirce had to think out a new term psychognosy. Something in between psychical and physical. Basic footing is on physics, but Peirce's account of mind has a visible unsound part for physicists. Peirce accepts mystic part intentionally in his account. It will only be understood when we see to his metaphysical scheme in chapter 5 below.

3-2 Dewey's Biological Monism

According to Darwinism, there is the principle of 'continuity' and 'emergence' in between a tuna and a human. Newtonian physics tried to afford unchanging laws of the nature in the fashion of deterministic closedness. Newtonian trend is no longer prevailing in modern science. However, cognitive science, i.e., A.I. is still struggling in the track of closed causality[30] business.

Perhaps it is now a time to look at a cult version of Dewey's account of mind. The aim of this section is to run a test for the 'usefulness'(this is what the term stands for after all) of pragmatistic metaphysics on a current issue of philosophy. Compared to the modern literature, Dewey's centenarian theory would look a bit too naive. Also Dewey's emergent theory of mind seem somewhat insufficient for the standard analytic philosophy. It would simply seem to be a mysticism of biology.

However, Dewey has his defence theory against such criticism. His defence theory is, at the same time, a criticism on traditional metaphysics and the method of science. It is a suggestion for a metaphysical reformation claiming that hitherto problem of philosophy is due to the mechanistic metaphysics and mechanistic materialism(by Dewey's term). The feature of pragmatism that I am to employ in the talk of philosophy of mind is Dewey's idea of new kind of materialism

---

30) Causality, here, means cause and effect principle that underlies in deterministic scheme of traditional science(science before modern time). Depending on causality, we are backed by completeness and certainty, but on the other hand, causality is only afforded in closedness at a cost of plasticity.

which he could only possibly afford under Peirce's so called 'speculative metaphysics.'[31]

Dewey is quite firm against the traditional mind/body dualism. It may be appropriate to begin with following passage of Dewey:

> The surrender is not easy of achievement. The philosophic tradition that comes to us from Classic Greek thought and that was reinforced by Christian philosophy in the middle ages discriminates knowing from other modes of knowing by means of an alleged peculiarly intimate concern with supreme, ultimate, true reality, To deny this trait to philosophy seems to many to be the suicide of philosophy; to be a systematic adoption of skepticism of agnostic positivism.[32]

Dewey considers Greek thoughts and Christianity as the main cause that mind/body problem is to be taken as metaphysical issue that strengthens the inbound system. Dewey's point is now to conceive matters of mind as outbound

---

31) Later, Whitehead called it "speculative idea" in meaning of adventuring of idea. Dewey called traditional philosophy a "spectator theory" meaning we, subject, the knower is watching fixed object, the theory known to earn one way diagram of knowledge which is insufficient.

32) John Dewey, *On Experience, Nature , and Freedom,* The Bobbs-Merrill Co. Inc., 1960, p. 58.

system of the traditional account and approach in scientific way. Dewey hopes his account of mind to be a contribution to the emergent theory of mind. He admits himself that his theory is rather crude and not elaborate enough, and furthermore the language he used in the theory was infected by the associations of old theories whose import is opposite to what he hoped to state:

> It may be conceived as an attempt to contribute to what has come to be called an 'emergent' theory of mind.[33]

And yet, Dewey's theory is clear enough to show his insight upon the features of mind(mind in general), an insight which gives us a fresh impact that no others have given. It is a doctrine based upon biology.[34] The theory begins with distinction between living and non-living things and, it follow up the stairs of hierarchical structure of organisms. Dewey's theory can be summarized as follows.

The most obvious difference between living and non-living

---

33) John Dewey, *Experience and Nature*, Open Court Publishing Co., 1926, p. 271,

34) Biology, here, stands against physics. Reductionists try to explain phenomena the closed-end physico-chemical reaction with causality, and in this way law or certainty can be afforded. Dewey and Peirce strongly oppose to reductionistic understanding of the world.

things is the character of their activity. The activity of the former is characterized by three terms; need, effect(or demand) and satisfaction. 'Need' stands for a condition of tensional distribution of energies of the body which is in a condition of uneasy or unstable equilibrium. 'Effect' or 'demand' stand for the manifested state of fact in movements which modify and environing bodies in ways to react upon the body to keep the characteristic pattern of active equilibrium.

'Satisfaction' stands for the recovery of this equilibrium pattern in react to the changes of environments caused by interaction between the demands of the body and environing bodies.

The need is not an immaterial or psychic force attached to matter, nor is it a notion or thought representing the difference between an state of need and a state of repletion of a organism.

> The need is neither an immaterial psychic force superimposed a notional or conceptual distinction, introduced by thought after comparison of two different states of the organism, one of emptiness and one of repletion.[35]

The term 'need' is employed here in strictly biological sense.

---

35) Ibid., p. 253.

It denotes a concrete state of events such as a tension in distribution of energy for high potential to low potential in accordance with the constantly altering environments. Up to this point, there is nothing that marks off non-living things from living things.

> In this fact, taken by itself, there is nothing which marks off the plant from the physico-chemical activity of inanimate bodies.[36)]

Dewey's strategy here is first to differentiate physico-chemical activity from plant which is lower life form than animate organic bodies. Dewey's theory structure is to take a hierarchical step up to the animate life form. The inanimate also undergoes reactions in relation to surrounding things in keeping the equilibrium until saturation terminates the cycle.

Physico-chemical activity of the inanimate iron is not distinguishable from physico-chemical activity of the animate plant.[37)] In both cases, the tensional distribution of energy is terminus at a point of 'saturation'. Thus, physico-chemical

---

36) Ibid., p. 253.

37) Plant, here, means ordinary vegetation that sprout out from seeds, grow and die. It does not mean any plant that has mobility or has some level of mental state.

'saturation' is the condition for the 'satisfaction'. Then, what makes an iron molecule and a plant differ? It is obvious that inorganic things such as iron are constituents of organic things. But it is also obvious that organisms are not just gathered cluster of inorganic parts. The difference is not that organisms have something additional to physico-chemical energy. The difference is that only organisms operate physico-chemical energy interconnected with complex integrated course or history. The main point to differentiate organism and inorganic is stated by Dewey as follows:

> For with animate bodies, recovery or restoration of the equilibrium pattern applies to the complex integrated course or history. In inanimate bodies as such, "saturation" occurs indifferently, not in such way as to tend to maintain a temporal pattern of activity.……Iron as such exhibits characteristics of bias of selective reaction, but it shows no bias in favor of remaining simple iron; it had just as soon, so to speak, become iron-oxide.[38)]

The Key word in above passage are 'history' and 'bias'. For organisms, equilibrium pattern is temporal in accordance to certain integrated conditions due to history, thus, the satisfactory

---

38) Ibid., p. 254.

physico-chemical 'saturation' point may differ in time and environment. A plant's animate activity involves its particular history along with basic physico-chemical need for survival. In inanimate iron molecule, undergoes physico-chemical reactions indifferently to meet the fixed 'saturation' point characterized by its identity. In a certain conditions iron becomes iron-oxide without a choice. Under such circumstance, becoming iron-oxide is to meet the physico-chemical 'saturation'. If an iron molecule exhibits a certain bias or selective tendency, it would be no longer inanimate.

> In the compound word, the prefix "psycho" denotes that physical activity has acquired additional properties, those of ability to procure a peculiar kind interactive support of needs from surrounding media.[39]

The peculiar property possessed by organism should be termed differently as "psycho-physical" activity. It should be noted here that both inanimate and animate things undergoes the consecutive activities of need-demand-satisfaction. Only that animate activity involves more complex operation effected by "psycho" which denotes the additional properties. It also should be noted that "psycho-physical" means not the mixture

39) Ibid., p. 255.

of the both, as a centaur is half man and half horse. It denotes the quality that the inanimate does not display. "Psycho" is not a term for something for beyond the present dimension or extra-material. It is a quality risen between physical activities.

For the activities of the constituent parts of an organism to conduce the perpetuation of patterned activity, there has to be bias of sensitivity. A part of organism is itself organized to maintain itself in its selective bias in interactions with the environments, at the same time, as to maintain the whole in which it takes its place. The operative relation of the whole in the part and of the part in the whole is what constitutes "susceptibility"(the capacity of feeling). Responses of an organism are not merely selective, but are discriminatory. The discrimination is the essence of sensitivity.

Organismic satisfaction is not a mere satiation of wants or repletion of need. It is rather difficult to see how sensitivity and interest are realized in sessile organisms. Because, a sensitivity realized in sessile organisms, generally speaking, does not seem to require premonition of what is to occur nor cumulation of what has occurred. However in animals with locomotion and distance-receptors, sensitivity seems to be realized as feeling.

As locomotion is vitally connected with space, locomotor

organs are accompanied by distance-receptors, and this implies the required time factor; the nearby means soon and the remote means later. The remote and the later give and effects of expectation or prediction to responses. Activities are thus differentiated by space-time condition into preparatory or anticipatory, and fulfilling or consummatory. Thus, in immediate response certain suffusion is resulted by the spatio-temporal factors. In such conditions sensibility is actualized as feeling to the useful and harmful surroundings which becomes premonitory in life. In the continuation of consummation or satisfaction of an organism, the culmination and the integrated cumulation sum up as a history, and thereby provides means through which the past can be made explicit without being revelled. For this characteristic of organism, feeling bears distinctions without end, and its existence is in a formless condition. Only with the growth of the multiplication of sensitive discriminations toward environment with the delicacy of organs inner movement(such as development of motor-organs with which internal granular organs react back and forth), complexity of quality and intensity of feelings grows.

An animal or a creature with complexity and activeness, would have that much feelings which vary abundantly in quality. But not until the creature is conscious about its own feelings it can be called "mental". Not every psycho-physical activity is mental. Mind is an added property assumed by a creature of feelings when the creature reaches to a point level where it acquired language or means of communication to interact with other living creature. Then the qualities of feeling can be at last become significant objective difference.[40)]

The distinctive qualities and efficacies of organisms are how these are specified by empirical events. There is no problem about the relation between "psychic" and "physical". The factual problem involved here is rather when and how exactly it is that an organization occur. There seems to be no satisfactory answer for this inquiry. Dewey stops his scientific inquiry at this point and accepts "psychical" turn out as natural phenomena that language of physics can not explicate, and writes:

> Organization is an empirical trait of some events, no matter how speculative and dubious theories about it may be; Especially no matter how false are certain doctrines about it which have had great vogue-namely, those doctrines

40) Subject of feeling act and react back and forth with object or other subject of feeling. John Dewey, "Nature, Life and Body-Mind," *Experience and Nature*, Open Court Publishing Co., 1926, ch. 7, pp. 249-271.

> which have construed it as evidence of a special force or entity called life or soul.[41)]

But the difficulty does not doom us in another philosophical mystery. No matter how vogue or false a speculative theories of organisms would be, namely those doctrines that attribute life or soul to be evidence of special force of organism, organisms are the only empirical trait of events from which we assume mental activities take places. Such construed character of organisms is indeed speculative, yet denying the sequential linkages of organismic events is more absurd. Denial of this speculation is not based on empirical evidence, but is a dialectical conclusion from a preconception.

The preconception is due to the mechanistic metaphysics, a belief that whatever comes later in time is less real, or in a complex of simplers, simplers are more real. But in the case of physics and biology Dewey seems to draw and strict line. Even though biology is on top of sharing domain with physics, Dewey seems to place biology beyond limit of physics. Thus, Dewey accepts the unanswered question of 'psycho' out of physico-chemical coordination and takes as natural character.

---

41) Ibid., p. 255.

3-3. Peirce's and Dewey's Defense Theory and Attack on Traditional Dualism

For the critics of Dewey's account of mind, Dewey gives a counter-criticism as defence theory. The argument attacks the traditional dualism and the scientific method. Dewey's argument to attack on the traditional dualism is as follows:

> We may reject the traditional dualism. In my conviction we should reject. We can not be scientific save as we seek for the physiological, the physical factor in every emotional, intellectual and volitional experience.[42]

The two greatest influential impetus to the general conception of human mind are the Greek metaphysics and its formalized version, the Cartesian dualism. Both suggested us a strict dualism which, in its extension to be referred to almost all human understanding of the world. The dichotomy of body and mind, matter and idea, temporal and eternal, contingent and universal, forms categories with which hierarchical arrangements and labels are fulfilled. Dewey says about Christian concept of mind body as follow:

---

42) John Dewey, *Intelligence in the Modern World*, The Modern Library, 1939, p. 827.

> In Pauline Christianity and its Successors, the body is early, fleshly lustful and passionate' spirit is Godlike, everlasting; flesh is corruptible, spirit incorruptible…… separation made in Christianity for practical moral purposes, between flesh and spirit sin and salvation, rebellion and obedience.[43)]

Thus in between the two criteria, body the lower and mind the higher, we take the world; appetite, temptation, corruption as the characters of body, and rational, ideal, moral as the profound nature of mind. By this diversity, not in nature but in human understanding of it, sciences have departed stressing only the latter in order to acquire certainty. Thenceforth, almost all human inquiries have been directed and infected by the dualistic metaphysics, the metaphysics originated from Greek thoughts.

For the problems of mind and body, some have accused Descartes for the charge of making the matter even more mysterious, certainly inadequate in dealing matters featuring characters that are beyond mechanistic principles. This accusation for Descartes is not fully binding because the

---

43) John Dewey, *Experience and Nature*, Open Court Publishing Co., 1926, p. 252.

substantial influence of the metaphysical scheme is originated in Plato's theory of 'Form' and its conclusive version, the Aristotelian metaphysical doctrine. In fact, Descartes only has culminated theories of feeling can be at last become significant objective difference.[44)]

The traditional dualism by formalizing it in more scrutinized form. Yet the salvation of Descartes from the charge should be limited only for metaphysics. Descartes' mechanistic explanation of the relation between mind and body layed out even a greater gorge between the two, instead of providing a solution. The attempt to explore the world made 'mind' even more mysterious thing. And the fellow investigators employed same method and even abused it in their work. The names of doctrines they hold are; interactionism, pre-established harmony, occasionalism, parallelism, pan-psychic idealism, epiphenomenalism…… a portentous array may go on and on. All they, whether dualism or not, are printed in the language of physics.[45)]

Now, from the two major fallacies in traditional thoughts, Dewey talks about the other is the scientific method for inquiry.

---

44) Ibid., p. 247.

45) In the current of philosophy of mind dualistic scheme underlies most literature. Dewey is a non-reductionistic monist. John Dewey, *Experience and Nature*, pp. 271~297.

What Dewey suggests is that having the restored metaphysical premise, we must employ a new method of inquiry that is not to hold on to causes but to start with the immediate qualities of the world, the events.

> It seems to me, accordingly, that the idiomatic use of the word "mind" gives a much more truly scientific, and philosophic, approach to the actual facts of the case than does the technical one.[46]

This idea of Dewey is also influenced by Peirce. Peirce claims that the problem is traditional method of inquiry "Cartesian Mistake"(CP 6, 42). Peirce claims that it is a unnatural doubt or inquiry to find out what the causes are. It is an inquiry just for the sake of the argument. For Peirce, doubt is not something we can will to exist. It is like pain and belief. Thus, Cartesian doubt for cause is not a natural one. The language is naturally designed to break down a cluster of body into grains in due course of seeking the cause. Then from the cause it remains as problem to reassemble the whole thing, not to mention to justify the cause itself. Dewey states this as follows:

46) John Dewey, *Intelligence in the Modern World*, The Modern Library, 1939, p. 811.

> ……the trouble lies not so much in the solution, as in the factors which determined statement of the problem. …… And these conceptions have primarily nothing to do with mind and body: they have to do with the underlying metaphysical issues:……the denial of quality in general to natural events; the ignoring in particular of temporal quality and the dogma of the superior the reality of "causes"?[47)]

The old determinism has collided to the obstacle of free-will and again the doctrine of free-will also is carried out by same rules of game and thus conclude the work with unfinished mysticism. Dewey on the other hand, gives us a totally new ground, ungrounded as seen by the prevailing stream of western analytic philosophy, a ground that treats the boundary between mind and body as nothing but a fiction, working out solely on material ground. For Peirce's and Dewey's counter criticism on traditional western system, they did not gain more or less no positive appeal to the whole crews and left out as side streamers for more than a century. At this point one may easily wonder how Chinese system of thoughts, metaphysics, and cosmology which are so interestingly sharing substantial common grounds with our early pragmatists, could so lively

47) John Dewey, *Experience and Nature*, Open Court Publishing Co., 1926, p. 252.

sustain in such a long time in their history. Their *li/chi* concept is neither moinism nor dualism. Our western analytic philosophy take either monism or dualism as a metaphysical ground. Philosophy of east and west are contrast at this point. And in Chinese epistemology, they draw a line on knowing at the line of *t'ai-chi* so that they can rest on their system accepting beyond the line of 'knowable' as mysteries. Thus, next chapter and on, Chinese thoughts on mind and metaphysical system and cosmology will be discussed along with Peircian and Deweian thoughts in order first to give a supporting power to the pragmatistic view of the world, and second, to give it a look and re-appreciation of the different systems in order to provide a room for crossing over of different systems that may blend out something new to crack out from the current holding point.

Chapter 4. Chinese Thoughts on Mind and Metaphysical Scheme:
Acceptance of the Limit of Knowing

It is not an easy task to make a visible comparison between western analytic philosophy and Chinese philosophy. However, in this chapter, I will first introduce Chinese traditional accounts on mind/body problem which are in similar context with western philosophy. Our interest is not in the various theories themselves but in their metaphysical ground. Although Chinese thoughts on mind are under certain logical set up, looking at them in the standard of *the law of causality of the west,* the base of Chinese epistemological system is unsatisfactory. It likely seems to end mystical for western method of causal deduction. Our interest on this matter is not to find out how mystical they are, but to see how Chinese thoughts on mind can rest on the seemingly mystical lay out on their metaphysical and epistemological ground. Therefore. I will deal with that discussion of rather a different philosophical system of China.

Second, we will look at *li/chi* concept that is, in western view, neither monism nor dualism. It shows a different kind of metaphysics against western standard. I hope that this *li/chi* concept gives a fresh impact to western traditional dualistic metaphysics in making a turning point.

Third, I will discuss *t'ai-chi* concept that is generally considered as 'Ultimate' in Chinese philosophy. *T'ai-chi* concept, similar to Tao concept, takes the world in two-fold mechanism; mundane, humanly, earthly world and the world beyond that. Mundane causal reductions in seeking answers stop right there in the line of *t'ai-chi*. *T'ai-chi* is somewhat like the western concept of god. This will be discussed in this chapter. We will see how Chinese could rest on unscientific or rather mystic theories on mind, as such as Peirce and Dewey do.

In Chinese philosophy, to talk about mind/body problem, *li/chi* concept must be brought out and *li/chi* concept will bring about *t'ai-chi* concept. The semi-dualistic *li/chi* concept[48] will be presented and discussed in terms of western dualistic epistemic stance. *T'ai-chi* concept will be compared with western causal reductionism.

In traditional western philosophy, generally mind and body

---

48) The term was used in Kim, Sang-Il, 金相日, *Whitehead and Eastern Philosophy*, Seo Guang Sa, 1993.

are two separately existing entities, and within mind, faculty of reason and other rest of faculties are conceived separately. In Chinese philosophy, mind seems to be taken as a set of sentiment as a whole and resides in body but not as a separate entity. Confucius, in *Lun-yü*(論語), stresses on hierarchical development of posterior psyche turn-out: *hsing-hsian-chin-hsi-hsiang-wuen*(性相近 習相遠).[49]

In the book of "*Lü-shih ch'un-ch'iu*", Human psyche developments are divided into three levels.[50] The first level is "*ching-ch'un* 精純". This level is purely material. When psyche is on matter "*ching-ch'un*" comes out meaning that one takes proper food, psyche resides on matter. The second level is "*ching-ch'i* 精氣". Vitality acquired by nourishment of material body becomes vitality of life. Up to this level, the theory itself is purely materialistic. At last, the third is "*ching-shen* 精神". In this last level, psyche that resides in mind becomes "spirit". It is a step by step elevation from matter to psyche. The elevation does not stop at a level of spirit. When one tries hard in "*kung-fu* 工夫", one might even get an ability to see the future.

49) Kim, Choong yeol, 金忠烈, "Introduction on Chinese Theory of Mind," Korean Association of Chinese Philosophy, *Substance and Mind in Chinese philosophy*, Yeon Sei Univ. Press, 1982.

50) Kim, Choong yeol, "Thoughts of Philosophy in the Chin Period," *Research of the Lü-shih ch'un-ch'iu*, Taiwan University Press, 1987, pp. 106-110.

Here, 工夫 means self-refinement.

When one becomes bright in spirit, one might be able to understand the nature of things to foresee the future. Here, I do not think the future telling is a kind of fortune telling in a circus. As mentality grow up high one might understand the part of world principle to know what will come to be in near future. This kind of understanding of the world in principle will be discussed in chapter 5.

This stepping up of psyche level of compound of materialism to mentalism has a hierarchical development of mentality that is quite compatible with that of Dewey's material monism discussed above. In Dewey's account too, the phenomena of psyche begins at a certain level of material. Dewey states that at a lowest level there is no difference between a plant and an iron particle, but at a certain level, life-forms and non-livings are differentiated.

It is stated above that at a level of '*ching-shen*', mind becomes spirit. I am not quite clear that what differences there are in between mind and spirit, but the important thing to notice here is that mind or spirit is emerged from material '*ching-ch'i*'. I would like to call this in western term: emergent theory of mind. At a certain level, it is not purely materialistic, and phenomena of psyche emerges on top of the material base.

Chinese theories about mind and that of Dewey's are both monistic in their structure but they are not entirely identical to western monistic theory of mentalism or materialism.

Kim, Choong yeol presents two contrasting theories about mind in his writing.[51] According to Kim, in the book of *T'ien-lun*(天論), Hsün-Tzu argues that mentality(心,神) emerges from prefixed material 'housing': *hsing-chü-erh-shen-sheng*(形具而神生, 天論, ch.17), so that body is prior to mind. This means that only after material body is formed mind resides on to it. On the contrary, a scholar of Han dynasty, Huan T'an argues, in the book of *Hong-ming-ji*(弘明集, bk.5), that mind is prior: *ching-shen-chü-hsing-t'i*(精神居形體), so that, mind is like a fire that burns wood or oil. In this case fire is prior to what are burned. When fire burns up wood or oil, fire can no longer be. Likewise, mind in a void without body is not possible. This also refers that there can be no such a thing as soul after death, once mind is off from a dead body.

Let us now take a look at Chu Hsi's account on mind. I will concentrate on Shu-Hsien Liu's interpretation. Liu has to say following in his opening words:

---

51) Kim, Choong yeol, "Introduction on Chinese Theory of Human Nature," Korean Association of Chinese Philosophy, ***Substance and Human Nature in Chinese Philosophy***, Yeon Sei Univ. Press 1982. In the quoted articles, the title of *Hong-ming-ji*, bk.5 is "***huan-jun-shan-hsin-lun-hsing-shen*** 桓君山新論形神".

> Chu Hsi, through a great many struggles in his thought finally arrives at the conclusion that the principles are static nature, only the mind is active and it embraces the principles.[52)]

We have to keep it in mind that the idea that mind is principle*(li)*. This means that mind is to be understood same as any other creative ontological principle of the universe. This was the prevailing thought of *Lu-Wang*. Chu Hsi's thought was different from the conventional thought that mind embraces various principles. In Chu Hsi's philosophy principle*(li)* and material force*(chi)* are not separable from each other. It is material force that realize principle to be actualized in this world. In this sense, principle is clearly ontologically prior, but at the same time without attachment to material force, principle will be of no ontic realization. This *li/chi* concept underlies Chu Hsi's account on mind. Liu interprets Chu Hsi's position as follows:

> It is clear that by following this line of thought Chu Hsi could not have taken the mind to be principle which is static in nature, as the mind is obviously as active agent.

52) Shu-Hsien Liu, "The Function of the Mind in Chu Hsi's Philosophy," *Journal of Chinese Philosophy 5*, D. Reidel Publishing Co., Dordrecht, Holland, 1978, p. 195.

> In fact Chu Hsi does maintain that the mind is the most refined and subtle kind of material force, and it has ability to penetrate into all principles.[53]

It is undeniable that Chu Hsi's account on mind is based on materialism. Thus, it should be our job to figure out how mind comes to be, in Chu Hsi's materialism. Chu Hsi's account on mind can be called, in modern term, a biological monism. Liu explains this in the following four headings:

> 1. …Chu Hsi does not mean that the mind is a creative ontological principle which is the source of all principles….
> 2. …Chu Hsi maintains that the mind embraces all principles…. Thus, mind and principle are two, but the relation between them is that of inherence. It is in this sense that from the very start they pervade each other.
> 3. The essence of the mind is that it can know principle and it can be master of itself, but in actuality it is often obstructed by selfish material desires endowed by material force….
> 4. It is here that we find distinction between the so-called moral mind and human mind. Moral mind is that which thoroughly conforms to principle, while human mind is that which mixes with physical endowment and human desires.[54]

---

53) Ibid., p. 197.

As we can see above number 4, for Chu Hsi, mind is on top of physical set up. The way he relates mind, desire and morality is similar to that of Hobbes. Allen Wittenborn points out that Chu Hsi's theory of mind is the least successful part of his otherwise masterly synthesis. Allen Wittenborn's point is that Chu Hsi had to cover too many functions of mind and had to deal with too many theories about mind; Mencius' notion of mind, features of the mind found in *Great Learning* and *Doctrine of the Mean,* elements from *Classic of Change* and so on. The result has been seen as frequent contradictory and inconsistency. However, Allen Wittenborn does not forget to mention that Chu Hsi was doing a theory of knowledge on a base of psychological foundation: in fact, he made one step advancement in Chinese philosophical psychology.[55]

We have seen so far that, in Chinese thoughts too, mind and body are discussed separately, and they cared about priority between mind and body. However, in Chinese thoughts, as we have seen above theories, mind and body are not ontologically dualistic.

Thereafter, in Chinese philosophy, mind or soul after death

---

54) Ibid., p. 198.

55) Allen Wittenborn, "Some Aspects of Mind and the Problem of Knowledge in Chu Hsi's Philosophy," *Journal of Chinese Philosophy 9*, Dialogue Publishing Company, Honolulu, Hawaii, 1982, pp. 13-14.

does not have much weight in philosophical discussion. This can be considered to be a result of pragmatic character of Confucianism. It is actually the matter of inward and outward in Chinese philosophy. Mind and body are not such divided two different ontological substances. The matter that concerns is see how mind takes perception of external world. P. T. Raju comments about Chinese concept of mind as follows:

> Nature for Chinese is the essence of man; and does not control; it, tempts to explain the material world and that in its term to explain inward…… It would therefore emphasize the control of inward first and that next the control of the outward.[56]

It is easy to notice that various sayings on mind/body problem in Chinese philosophy are running in different channels. However one thing we may point out from Chinese philosophy is that they are rather in the side of monism. Different theories can meet at the point that mind and body are not separable. No matter which is prior, in theories, mind and body go together. This near-monistic view of mind/body can be compared with *li/chi* concept which shares common

---

56) P. T. Raju, *Introduction to Comparative Philosophy*, University of Nevbraska Press, 1962, p. 98.

structure of ontology. It may be either *li* is prior to *chi* or *chi* is prior to *li*, but *li and chi* are always together as substance.

According to Wen-shan Huang, in "*t'ien hsia* 天下", there are *li* and *chi; li* is '*Tao*' of metaphysical world and base of the all things and *chi* is base of the mundane world. Everything comes to be with innate *li* and only when *chi* is acquired a thing can have a form. In this view, *li* and chi are together dualistic and can be compared to the concept of Platonic dualism of form and matter. But at the same time, *li/chi* concept is not as dualistic as the western concept. There are various theories about *li* and *chi* in Chinese philosophy. Theories are generally divided into two groups: one that takes *li* prior and the other that take *chi* prior.

In Han Dynasty, *chi* was taken prior, and *t'ai-chi* is *chi* of chaos in that *yin*(陰) and *yang*(陽) are not yet divided. *Li* can be explained as property of *chi* that is the principle of all changes. Chu Hsi and Ch'eng I later took *li* prior that chi is something tamed and controlled by *li*. In this system, if we pull time factor into it, *li* comes to be prior to *chi*. But either cases, *li* or *chi* can not come to be an existence alone. This is the point we should pay our attention. The western dualism is something quite apart from *li/chi* concept. *Li/chi* concept has character of both dualism and monism.[57]

Chu Hsi, on one hand, says that *li* and *chi* are separately existing and, on the other hand, the two are in their peculiar relation to be as one. In the relation between *li* and *chi* no matter which comes to be taken as prior, the two are not to be taken dualistic, in western standard. Wen-shan Huang explains this in a rather modern term as follows:

> The dualistic philosophy reigned supreme in Western thought dominating the development of science. But with the advance of atomic physics, findings on demonstrable experiment, were seen to negated the dualistic theory and the trend of modern thought then has led back towards the monistic theory of I Ching and the conception of the Taoists.[58)]

Modern discoveries in Western science may help in discussing old Chinese thoughts. But in principle, we should notice, the old Chinese thoughts initially has different footing of conceiving the world. In thinking of *li/chi* concept we should learn the epistemic attitude that adopt and accept the idea of oneness within the scheme of many separated things. To have the idea affirmable in the system of the West, a new term had

57) Wen-shan Huang, "T'ai Chi Ch'uan and I-Ching, or the book of the Changes," *Chinese Philosophy*, Vol.1, China Academy, 1974.

58) Ibid., p. 403.

to be invented to call "two and two in one": semi-dualism.

Even in Chinese philosophy there is a trial of reduction to find out the principle causation of the world. But the reduction ends quickly instead of going ad-absurdum. The two primal force of the world: *yin* and *yang* are from the Supreme Ultimate(太極). And in Chinese philosophy deducive reduction ends right at the level of *t'ai-chi*. Tat Wei explains the idea of *t'ai-chi* from the *I Ching* as follows:

> The book teaches us that there exists one Boundless Immutable Principle, one absolute Reality, which antecedents all manifested conditioned Being. It is called in the I Ching the t'ai-chi, i.e., Supreme Ultimate. This Ultimate Reality is the One life, the one Self Existence, the Absolute all in all, eternal and infinite, the causeless…[59]

As we can see from the passage above, *t'ai-chi* is the biggest concept in Chinese metaphysics. *T'ai-chi* is the fundamental causation of the world, so that, the questioned reduction to acquire the origin of the universe ends at the line of *t'ai-chi*. Chou Tun-i borrowed the term "*wu-chi* 無極" from Lao Tzu chapter 28, and set forth prior to *t'ai-chi*[60]. If *wu-chi* is prior

59) Tat Wei, "Confucius and I-Ching," *Chinese Philosophy*, Vol. 1, China Academy, 1974.

to *t'ai-chi*, it would mean that Taoists' metaphysical concept ontologically prior to Confucian concept. *wu-chi* is taoists concept and *t'ai-chi* is a Confucian concept.

It is interesting that later Chu Hsi resets the relation between *wu-chi* and *t'ai-chi*. Chu Hsi set *wu-chi* not on top of *t'ai-chi* but in parallel position[61)], so that, he took *wu-chi* as something like *t'ai-chi's* adjective. Thus, thereafter in Chinese philosophy and in Confucian school, became the concept of the 'ultimate principle.' *T'ai-chi* is the end of reduction. Chinese philosophy has drawn the line right there at *t'ai-chi*. Of course, there is idea of indefinite universe, but in Chinese cosmology, there also is drawn a line for something in our interest, and other world are not our immediate interest according to the drawn line of *t'ai-chi*. James R. Ware speaks of this matter as follows:

> We conclude therefore, that in every analysis there is something not subject to argument, If you are still in doubt, I can only say that the sage cherishes the topic in his bosom(he knows intuitively) …knowledges is at its peak when it stops with that it does not know. Who really understands the argument that used no words, or the

---

60) Man-jan Cheng, *Lao-Tzu "My words are very easy to understand,"* ch. 28, trans. by Tam C. Gibbs, North Atlantic Books, 1981.

61) Wen-shan Huang, "T'ai Chi Ch'uan and I-Ching, of the Book of the Changes," *Chinese Philosophy*, Vol.1, China Academy, 1974.

utterance that does no articulating?[62]

From *t'ai-chi* concept, it is not difficult to notice that Chinese philosophy in general draw line of interest limited in this life. It is also not difficult to see that their cosmology includes the unlimited expansion of the universe. But they draws a line of inquiry right at *t'ai-chi*. *T'ai-chi* concept has to provide all the principal answers of the world. And Chinese in general are satisfied with it. Western cosmology is not limited in '*t'ien-hsia* 天下' earthly life so that our inquiry in the form of causal reduction meets at its limit of knowledge.

Chinese philosophy seems to start from a quite different set up. Their interest is limited in the world of '*t'en-hsia* 天下' and in this earthly life. Even though they have inquiry on vast universe and eternity. How did they limit their interest in this limited earthly life? Taoists put it in twofold vision; one earthly *Tao* and the other un-namable true *Tao*. But the greatest influence of all is Confucian concept of *t'ai-chi*. Confucian concept of *t'ai-chi* handles the protruding inquiries of causal reduction for the origin of the world. In this limited space, life and time are the factors that gives openness for the future. Life is short but life continuously goes on life after life. Chinese

62) James R. Ware, *The Saying of Chuang-Tzu* a new Translation, Confucius Publishing Co., 1959. p. 22.

find themselves unlimited world vision in this limited cosmology. *T'ai-chi*, thus has the Ultimacy of principle and Supremacy that puts down causal reductionism. There is no 'must' in taking one's own epistemic stance. Western philosophy took their way, and Chinese philosophy took theirs and satisfied in their own way. I now say that epistemic stance should be taken as an 'attitude' not as any causal result.

Chapter 5. Epistemology, East and West

In chapter 5 epistemology and metaphysics will be discussed. We need to discuss how two scientists, Peirce and Dewey, in scientific approach on mind, present such unscientific and indeterministic theories on mind. Their indeterminism was long before the later scientists of quantum physics, Louis de Broglie, Prigogine open a new era of indeterministic concept of the universe. Here, I argue that it is due to their epistemic stance and metaphysical ground that they set out their arguments.

Murray G. Murphey explains intellectual and scientific flow of the late 19th century as follows:

> The reign of Newtonian mechanics was rapidly drawing to a close, and many of the fundamental difficulties were already known……The projection of general evolutionary cosmologies was not a new undertaking in this period. Herbert Spencer, and John Fiske, and Frank Abbot, to mention only a few obvious examples, had already tried their hands at such a task. But such theories were so

largely fanciful and so clearly nonscientific that scientists themselves remained highly skeptical. It was Peirce's endeavor to build a cosmological theory which would be broad enough to afford a view of the probable course of future events yet specific enough to be scientifically acceptable.[63]

The regime of Newtonian deterministic cosmology seemed to be on it's downward direction at the end of 19th century. And the traditional scientific attitude of pursuing unchangeable, fixed and static answer about the nature started to be challenged other new visions.

Peirce starts out pointing out that the universe is too vast to have character and what we think of true is noting but opinions. In the first section, Peirce's theory of knowing will be discussed in depth, Dewey argues that knower and known are in two-way relation and everything around knowing is interwoven and continuously interact. Peirce's cosmology of Tychism/Synechism will be compared with Lao Tzu's double aspects of *Tao*. Different understandings on *Tao* in various writings will be included in this chapter.

One thing is clear about those concepts upon *Tao* that there

---

63) Murray G. Murphey, *The Development of Peirce's Philosophy*, Hackett Publishing co., inc. Indianapolis/Cambridge, 1961, pp. 327-329,

is sustaining dualism that one concept of *Tao* is about the mundane world of which we can normally gain knowledge about, and the other is true eternal *Tao* which is beyond the reach of our sensory perception. This dualistic feature of *Tao* can be compared with Peirce's dualistic acceptance of the world; one part that we can have knowledge of; Synechism, and the other that we have no knowledge of; Tychism. The discussion will be focused on Peirce's Tychism, event without causal antecedent, and Lao Tzu's 'being from non-being'.

Next, Dewey's and Chuang Tzu's epistemology will be discussed. The key point of Dewey's and Chuang Tzu's epistemology; 'comprehensively harmonized monism', is that the knower; subject, is not separated from the object but embraced by surrounding environment. In other words, we are commingled in this ever changing world so that we are actually within the objects of our perception. Dewey's holistic system of knowing will be discussed and, in the end, Dewey's view will be briefly compared with Chuang Tzu's epistemology of 'comprehensively harmonized monism'.

In this system of metaphysics and epistemology we make a notice on two things. First, through Peirce's and Lao Tzu's metaphysics, there is a line in perception of the world beyond which we may not normally attain knowledge through sensory perception. And second, Dewey and Chuang Tzu are similar in their monistic epistemology. Both will agree on the point that there is no static thing in this world. And in this continuously changing world there is no division between subject and object.

- Peirce's Theory of Knowledge -

Just by taking a glance at Peircian and Deweian arguments one might think that Peirce or Dewey employed Chinese metaphysics. It will not be possible to find that out or prove it, but it is worse while to discuss these in a linear set up.

First, to recapture the originating ideas of Charles Sanders Peirce from the misleading concepts around Anglo-American analytic philosophy. Thus, I will present the doctrine of pragmatism focusing on Peirce's theory of truth and metaphysical scheme. My intention here is to crystallize the core of pragmatic perspective in order to elevate pragmatism to a pure philosophic conduct. For this intention, I will not endorse the true heritage of pragmatism to William James. A brief comparison between James and Peirce will be included. We can not just disregard the relation between our common usage of the notion and James' version of pragmatism. We have to keep it in mind the traditional Western epistemology of causality as reading this section to see the great diversity with Peircian system.

The colloquial English word "usefulness" used by some early proprietors of pragmatism rendered an overestimated allowance for the usage of the word. If pragmatism takes 'usefulness' or 'practical bearing'(it was seen so by others) as a criteria of judgment for the business of the living that is vigorous, unstable and superbly flexible by nature, it would be a commitment to a "uselessness."

Peirce's statements on pragmatism would be all together an argument that has one large outset with the least coherency. The material is not entirely comprehensive, but I will try to extract the core in order to understand his opinion on 'knowing' ,'truth' and 'the world'. Peirce's pragmatism is considered to be a 'maxim' or 'method to clarify idea', or is called 'theory of meaning' by himself. It is a maxim of ascertaining sign(or term). But not all signs are of his interest. Peirce says:

> "The method of determining the meaning of intellectual concepts that is, of those upon which reasoning may turn."(CP 6, 8)

The theory of meaning would not concern ubiquitous

meaning nor ordinary communication. It applies to what Peirce calls "intellectual purport" of words. Thus the rule of Peirce's pragmatism begins with procedural rule to clarify meanings of certain class of signs which is necessary for communication in knowledge. However, in Peirce's theory of meaning, it is not clear what this 'meanings' nor the adequate 'methods' is. But one point is clear by the statements;

> Our idea of anything is our idea of sensible effects.(CP 5, 401) The whole conception of this quality, as of every other, lies in its conceived effects.(CP 5, 403)

The first statement looks like a Berkeleian idealism. It implies that an idea which is receipted senses upon a thing is a person's own and is apart from the thing-itself. And the latter implies that an idea upon a thing may differ due to each cumulating sensible effects. There can be variance of quality acquired by sensible effects each case of time by each receiptor. These uneasy premises make the task of gaining meanings and communication with them a very difficult job. The 'signs' from Peirce are not necessarily words. Peirce's sign includes whatever means that can convey such as symbols, picture, or even gesture. Of all the signs, words are the most affordable ones so that Peirce's method of clarifying meaning suggests an analyzed way of using words. This is done something like the following:

> If T1(hard)=T2, and T2=S, if S is such and such ExpS, and if O(scratching test), than R(will not be scratched).[64]

Here, 'Exp' means 'experience'. The above method of describing meaning is later formalized and earned popularity by Ramsey and Lewis. The example Peirce brought out was the idea of 'hardness'. The sign 'hard' means, somehow, "will not be scratched". Then, we have to see if that meaning is confirmable by experiments. Now, there is an indefinite number of possible confirmable consequences. But the notable point here is that Peirce is saying that we can clearly say that 'X is hard' if we fail to scratch 'X' every time we tried, without going through all the indefinite number of testing. This sounds like the idea of the verification theory of Carnap that comes out three dozen some years later. But the crucial difference between Carnap and Peirce is that Peirce takes the meaning as a subclass meaning of the sign and the total sum of actuality can be otherwise. Knowing a meaning, for Peirce, involves a commitment to an unconquerability of 'indefinite series' of

64) H. S. Thayer, "Pragmatism," *A Critical History of Western Philosophy*, Macmillan, 1964.

confirming instances.

From the passage above, we can reckon that Peirce must have quite different perspective on truth. Peirce regards both 'believing A' and 'thinking that A is true' as same mental acts. Our thoughts are clusters of belief or concept. But not all belief share same characteristic. A certain characteristic such as right or wrong can be attached only to a certain kind of belief such of science. Which belief is true or which belief is false is a matter to be determined on the ground whether the belief actually coincides with the fact. Thus truth, says Peirce:

> ...is accordingly conceived as a characteristic of belief we would possess if it were affected by nothing but the rea l⋯.(CP 5, 384)

This is, in other words, truth is a belief which represents a real object.[65] Peirce's account on truth can be well represented by following two sentences:

> The opinion which is fated to be ultimately agreed upon by all who investigate is what we mean by truth, and the object represented by this opinion is real(CP 5, 407)

65) Dewey later took this account and claimed his theory is the only true correspondence theory of truth.

> Truth is that concordance of an abstract statement with the ideal limit toward which endless investigation would tend to bring scientific belief, which concordance the abstract statement may possess by virtue of the confession of its inaccuracy and one-sidedness, and this confession is an essential ingredient of truth.(CP 5, 565)

By these two statements, Peirce earned various criticism. Truth, by the definition, is a certain opinion which would be ultimately agreed and is concordance of statement which endless investigation would bring belief. Russell argues for this in chronological sense that a terminal A-bomb warfare would falsify the definition because there will be no man left to investigate nor to agree each other.[66] In this, square-minded Russell is misleading Peirce's assertion and this kind of misleading would not be so unnatural for analytic philosophers of the day.

Truth is something we 'would agree' not 'will agree'. There is an important difference between 'would' and 'will'. 'Will' is definite and 'would' is not. If we say "it will be true" than this means it will definitely be true some time in the future no matter what happens. But if we say "it would be true", in this statement, there are hidden 'ifs'; if the premises are correct, if the course

66) *Philosophy of John Dewey*, Evanston and Chicago, 1939, p. 144.

does not change, if everything will be as we expect now, and so on. In Peirce's assertion, truth is what we 'would' agree and this does not entail the future act of some living men's agreement nor the actual evidence that it surely turn out as a truth.

Peirce's definition of truth is thus an 'indefinite' definition. Peircian notion of truth is indeed quite apart from the main streamers. The underlying assumptions is that our knowledge about the world is only partial, and even if we attain the total sum data of the universe we can not have one solid truth about it because the universe is endlessly eminence; it is not a blocked object. Within this kind of metaphysical scheme which might not seem so bright for some scientific enthusiasts, Peirce claims that his method is a pragmatic way of attaining knowledge.

Peirce's maxim as he called his methods of analysis, became James' "universal mission"[67]. Peirce's suggestion of confirming the usage of sign for the ultimate agreement for investigators became converted into an evaluation of moral, psychological and social effect of ideas in James' system. The term "agreement" plays a big part is James' system. And the best way to attain agreement would be to look the "cash value". Truth, says James "is whatever proves itself to be good in the way of belief."[68]

---

67) William James, *Pragmatism*, Logman's Green, New York, 1907. p. 2.

68) Ibid., p. 222.

'True', 'good', and 'value' are all plastic matter. And as an empiricist, James believed that 'good' can only be tested by 'result'. So, it can be interpreted as; "whatever works is good and unless it is proven useful we do not know". This should be the motto of James' radical empiricism. James wanted his doctrine to be a revision of J. S. Mill's Utilitarianism. So much difference we see between Peirce; the initiator, and James; the publisher[69]. For this reason Peirce renamed his original position "pragmaticism" "a word ugly enough", says Peirce, "to be safe from the kidnappers".(CP 5, 403)

Much of our talk of pragmatism is of James' version. As Dewey puts Peirce, a logician, and James, a humanist, these two acquainted men, even though they exchanged a number of comments each other, end up so much diverse upon the single term; 'pragmatism.' To decide which one to be the legitimate one for the sole terminology is a problem to be debated else-where. My task in this book is to discuss the Peircian

---

69) The notion of pragmatism was first announced by James' address at University of California at Berkeley in 1898. The original term of Peirce, as he claims, was from Kant's term 'pragmatisch' meaning experiencing of testing. Peirce first thought of the idea of pragmatism when he was reading Kant's *The Critique of Pure Reason*. Peirce was against Kant for 'noumena' and 'synthetic a priori'. Peirce's anti-Kantian or anti-representationalism lives on in American intellectual followed by Dewey, Whitehead, Quine……etc. James' term, on the other hand, was originated from 'Pragma' of Greek, meaning practice.

pragmatism(P–pragmatism I might call). Peirce's opinion on truth and knowledge is largely overshaded by James'. The reason I can think of is that James' is much easier to comprehend. Then, the reason could be the complexity of Peirce's metaphysics, his vision toward the universe.

In metaphysics, we talk about the 'world' and 'I'. At the bottom of human thought, it is a clear fact that 'I' is the 'knower' and the 'world' is 'To know'. Thus, any opinion on 'knowledge' should be on and opinion on the relation between the 'world' and 'I'. This ground job for human knowledge is a major task of metaphysics. Peirce's metaphysics is a unique one. Peirce characterizes the universe as follows:

> The universe ought to be presumed too vast to have any character.(CP 6, 422)

All the pictures about the universe, from the Church, from the Greeks, or from the science, are one drawn upon their wish. Peirce says:

> scientific presumption is that the unknown parts of space and time are like the known parts.(CP 6, 421)

The scientific mind tries to mold solid knowledge about unknown by the rules of known. Mystical mind does the same but only by the rules of unknown. Peirce thinks both are irrelevant to deal with the uncharacterisible universe. Peirce says, as a scientist, "But there are better minds who take up mystical theories(by which I mean all those which have no possibility of being mechanically explained)"[70]. This is a crucial point that Peirce's universe is so big and complex that no single language can describe the nature of it. In fact, Peirce's universe has so many characters, characters that are organismic, that no single solid character exists.[71] Now, if we get back to his definition of truth, we can see how the statement works in accordance with his vision of the universe. The reality of the world is, in principle, not fully attainable.

The term 'truth' is only a name of an ideal phantom, there is no such a thing in the world. But, this does not make Peirce a skeptic. He believes the science is on its way to the truth,

---

70) C.P. 6, 422 But, by this, Peirce would not mean any mysticism such as witchcraft, totemism, or religious myth.

71) This view of Peirce became a philosophical ground for Dewey. And a great similarity is found in Whitehead's philosophy. Dewey used the term 'biological phase' and Whitehead(in his works in Harvard) used 'organic universe' and 'speculative metaphysics'. The terms and notion are much popular today specially in the field of astronomy(the living universe) and computer science and cognitive science(biological solution in understanding of human brain).

only that the 'truth' Peirce means is a lesser truth compared to the idealists' so that the ideal truth will not be met. Thus, Peirce's method should be a pragmatic method to do the work of science. The important point for us to carry on our way to the discussion of philosophy of mind is that the world is not entirely mechanistic.

Modern philosophy initiated by Descartes was to do away with mystery and secure the certainty for our intellectual construction. Cartesian dualistic metaphysics divides the world into two: physical and non-physical. Inspired by the fruitfulness of natural science on top of the Cartesian metaphysics, our intellectual pursue endorsed the language of physics the only legitimate apparatus of science. Deconstructionism, a breed of the post-modernistic wave, directly opposes such construction of intellectual enterprise. Some takes pragmatism as an American reflection for the deconstructionism. But this is not quite true. Pragmatism is indeed not modernistic, but is not a skepticism, nor an epistemological anarchism. Pragmatisitc method is not for any deconstructionism. It is a method of 'maker', only with a wider plan.

Peirce's 'speculative metaphysics' give us a new perspective upon the world. It makes our environment of science much more comfortable for the dilemmas risen by the limit of physical language. Peirce's theory of 'Fallibilism'(from his definition of truth) give us a way out for such dilemmas of science as theory of quantum mechanic and double aspect of light which directly challenge coherency of the existing principles of physics. For Peirce, mysticism is all right. A mystery could be just another character of the universe. *A part for Ford can be a mystery for G. M. plant.* Speculation is also all right and induction is also acceptable for Peirce. Only that neither can be definite.

As we have seen above, Dewey also warns the mechanistic metaphysics and the sole usage of physical language. Dewey's philosophy of mind is biology oriented. He opposes the reduction of biology to physics. An organism in constitute of inorganic parts, but that is not all that makes it a living. The difference between a dead amoeba and a live one is the power of 'life', and that is the core of biology. Thus, biology includes physics but not reducible to it. The mystic power of life in biology is a 'mystery' to physics.

The character of current biology lies on its tendency toward microcosm. It tend to find answers for 'life' from the microcosmic world. The in-organic universe is big and life forms are tiny. The biggest life form in the universe we can think of for now would be about seaquaya trees[72]. They tried to find any trace of life forms when they first lend on the Moon and Mars. What they looked for was nothing but an Earthian microcosmic biological standard of organism. However, if we take off from this position and take the modern astronomical view, the whole universe is one big living entity. Even in the macrocosmic world, there are birth, growth, and death of stars and galaxies. The universe is one big organism for 'macrocosmic biology'. This view would be the interpretation of Peirce's idea of 'organismic cosmos'. And thus, any talk of this organismic entity should ultimately be a talk of biology.

Now, if we get back to the table of philosophy of mind bearing the Peircian speculation and Deweian idea of biological approach, we will be more comfortable to endorse the character of plasticity emerging from the construction of closed mechanism. As we have seen above, the crucial characteristic difference between mental and physical: qualia, fallibility, semantic ability, intentionality, self-correctability, and ability to learn……etc, are after all due to closedness of cause and effect mechanism. Unless we resolve these problems, mind will remain as an 'inexistence' in the physical world. But, if we endorse plasticity that somehow emerges on top of a physical

---

72) A kind of tree grow in North-Western America. Considered to be the biggest and oldest life form in earth. Some are over 5000 years old.

construction, everything will remain as physical and some of them may have the option of biological character.

The closedness of cause and effect chain is a constraint of physical rule. If we expand our field of conduct to the biological ground as Dewey suggests, the closedness problem may be resolved. But then, biology can only be the rule of the livings. Thus, if we accept Peirce and Dewey's system, from then on, our problem on mind will be to solve the mystery of 'life'. By fixing our mechanistic metaphysics, hinted by the core features of pragmatism, we might have some forwarding momentum in our endeavor of exploring human mind. Then, all Ideas for devising a thinking machine will always be byproducts of the understanding of the brain act. We must first know how the brain or mind is, what it is like, before we discuss anything at all about simulating it.

- Metaphysical System: Peirce and Lao Tzu -

One of the aim of this chapter is to make an alinement between Peirce's Tychism/Synechism and Lao Tzu's dual aspects of *Tao*. Peirce's view on dual aspects of the world is well illustrated in his cosmology of Tychism/Synechism. An event without causal antecedents is what we can not know or explain away. Peirce calls this 'Tychism' and takes it as true feature of the universe. What we can normally know in sensory perception; the habit-taking features of the world, Peirce calls it 'Synechism'.

Lao Tzu opens *Tao-te Ching* saying '*Tao-ke-Tao-fei-Ch'ang Tao* 道可道 非常道' The first kind of *Tao* is of our mundane world that we can say about. And the latter *Tao*(*Ch'ang Tao* 常道) is something we can not perceive with our ordinary sense. It will be an interesting and challenging task to make an alinement between Tychism/Synchism and 常道(*Ch'ang Tao*)/道(*Tao*). My strategy here is not to deal with embracing vision of the holistic universe, but to make a visible appreciation on both Peirce's and Lao-Tzu's epistemic attitude that differentiate what we can normally know and what we can not.

Darwinian concept of evolution shades over Peirce's cosmology. Peirce's evolutionary universe must have dual aspects; continuity and emergence. Two are the needs for evolution. Evolution means change and it is the character of organismic universe. Dual aspects of universe in Peirce's term, are continuity and absolute chance. Continuity must have a factor of habit-taking regularity and absolute chance means event without causal antecedents. For things or events without causal antecedents are, in common term, 'new', conceived as new in course continuous show down of things or events.

> I have begun by showing that Tychism must give birth to an evolutionary cosmology, in which all the regularities of nature and of mind are regarded as products of growth··· (CP 6, 102)

In the universe there are both regularity and new things, but it seems in Peirce's view, new things are prior with time factor and thus give birth to all regularities in nature. Peirce's doctrine of absolute chance is real feature of Universe and he calls it Tychism from a Latin word meaning 'Chance'.

> Thus was born Peirce's famous theory of Tychism, or absolute chance. Although the doctrine was not formulated until the late eighties of early nineties, its origins can be traced back to some of Peirce's earlier writings. It was probably the question of the validity of induction which first led Peirce to stress the disorderliness of the universe[73)]

In a deterministic scheme of cause all effect, every posterior events is not considered to be 'new' because it is definitely comes to be in the line of time factor. In the mechanism of

---

73) Murray G. Murphey, *The Development of Peirce's Philosophy*, Hackett Publishing Co. Inc. Indianapolis/Cambridge. 1961, p. 333.

deterministic changes things are meant to be in regularity. No new things. For the concept of evolution Peirce must hold on to the concept of real chance: doctrine of Tychism.

> In short, if we are going to regard the universe as a result of evolution at all, we must think that not merely the existing universe, that locus in the cosmos, to which our reactions are limited, but the whole Platonic world, which in it self is equally real, is evolutionary in its origin, too..... ......The very first and most fundamental element that we have to assume is a Freedom, or chance, or Spontaneity.....(CP 6, 200)

Evolution is real character of universe and can only be afforded when there is Freedom or chance for a new thing. Without the feature of evolution or real chance the world would be perfectly deterministic and the real feature of granular things must be static. The meaning of change is not merely change in shape. Changes must include the factor of 'something new in time', the real chance.

> Let me have say one word about Tychism, or the doctrine that absolute chance is a factor of the universe. There in one class of objecters to it who are impressed with what they have read in popular books about the triumphs of

science that they really imagine that science has proved that the universe is regulated by low down to every detail.(CP 6, 201)

By 'popular books', Peirce must have meant the sources of conventional Newtonian physics. Our glance on the macro-scopic cosmology suggested deterministic administration of the system. Planets' orbital movements are observed in a quite deterministic mechanism related to gravity and velocity. Popular science, for the time being, were being developed in such track of mechanism at the era of Peirce. Peirce argues pre-causal nature of the universe. In the time of Peirce and even nowadays, a little fact from scientific discovery may cause total alteration or abandonment of an existing system of metaphysics.

Using a scientific information, Peirce stress on real chances of the universe:

> …it will be simplest to remark that physicists hold that the particles of gases are moving about irregularly, substantially as if by real chance and that by the principles of probabilities there must occasionally happen to be concentrations of heat in the gases contrary to the second law of thermodynamics….(CP 6, 47)

In above passage, Peirce discusses principle of probability and the second law of thermodynamics in terms of irregularity. It is interesting fact that it was a half century before Prigogine discusses seriously about the law of entropy. This doctrine of real chance explains the nature of evolution of the universe. In this system, events without causal antecedent, the unexplainables are the real features of the nature. The novelty of the universe can not be explained. It is the ultimate aspect of the world. But then, a question remains as, "How do we get our knowledge for the nature?" It is not difficult to accept Peirce's doctrine of real chance, but giving up the whole system of knowledge is another story. And also, for evolution, there need to be continuity along with real chance.

> Peirce's doctrine of continuity(generality, law, regularity), he called Synechism. Thus, Tychism and Synechism are opposing principle, yet Tychism gives birth of new uniformities and Synechism is never entirely free of chance.[74)]

When everything is in real chance we may call it 'chaos'. However, we must experience a certain level of ordered driving

---

74) John K. Sheriff, *Charles Peirce's Guess at the Riddle*, Grounds for Human Significance, Indiana Univ. Press, 1994, pp. 92-93.

force in the nature to attain certain level of uniformities for any knowledge to grow.

> In doing this, I shall for the time drop my Tychism out of view, in order to allow a free and independent expansion to another conception··· most indispensible to philosophy, though it was not there dwelt upon; I mean the idea of continuity. The tendency to regard continuity, in the sense in which I shall define it, as an idea of prime importance in philosophy may conveniently be termed Synechism.(CP 6, 103)

There is the tendency to regard continuity. There are also habit-taking features in the nature of universe. This doctrine is called 'Synechism'. Continuity means a succession of novel events. Regularities grow from continuous succession. The universe might seem ordered.

> In fact we are thus brought close to the doctrine of Synechism, which is the elements of thirdness cannot entirely by escaped.(CP 6, 653)

Tychism is a doctrine for absolute chance which accounts for 'new' or 'chance' of the nature. And Synechism is for seemingly regularity of the nature; habit-taking features of the nature. Peirce's conception upon the world is three fold; firstness, secondness and thirdness. These terms identify 'quality', 'reaction' and 'generality'. Peirce holds onto both real chance and continuity of the world. And in between the two 'reaction' takes part as mediation. The world is not entirely filled with real chances and at the same time not entirely mechanical.

> Those observations which are generally adduced in favor of mechanical causation simple prove that there is an element of regularity in nature, and have no bearing whatever upon the question of whether such regularity is exact and universal or not. ……Try to verify any law of nature, and you will find that the more precise your observations, the more certain they will be to show irregular departures from the low.(CP 6, 46)

Above passage of Peirce can be analyzed that to the down-low micro-scopic way things are irregular and that irregularity is the departure. Up-high macro-scopic way things look more regular in order. Thus, basically Peirce accept both irregularity and appearing regularity of the nature. And law of nature can be acquired in the three fold conceptual set up:

> Permit me further to say that I object to having my

> metaphysical system as a whole called Tychism. For although Tychism does enter into it, it only enters as subsidiary to that which is really, as I regard it, the characteristic of my doctrine, namely, that I chiefly insist upon continuity, or thirdness, and, in order to secure to thirdness its really commanding function.(CP 6, 202)

In Peirce's system of conception, Tychism takes only subsidiary part. It seem, even though it is, attached feature on nature itself, thirdness takes an major roll in conception. Therefore, conceived features of the nature are of those that occur in succession with human effort of conceiving. Thirdness is what we conceive from nature's seeming habit-taking fcatures.

> At any rate, it is clear that nothing but a principle of habit, itself due to growth by habit of an infinitesimal chance tendency toward habit-taking, is the only bridge that can span the chasm between the chancemedly of chaos and the cosmos of order and low.(CP 6, 262)

Peirce disavows the concept of 'certainty' of nature. The closest terms that Peirce gives are habit-taking or regularity of the nature. In the doctrine of Tychism alone, there only is real chance; chaos. But in the doctrine of Synechism habit-taking regularity grows. Upon those habit-taking features of the universe we attain knowledge, and as the universe organismically grows so does our knowledge

The key concept of Peirce's Tychism is 'novelty'. Of absolute chance, there is no causal antecedent to be truly 'new'. Having no antecedent does not necessarily means no antecedent at all. It is the case that novelty has no causal chain, one can not tell or foretell about such event. In other words, whether there is a antecedent or not, we can not know about it in our sens perception. We can only know about continuously habit-taking event, Synechism. One point we ought to bear in moving onto concept of *Tao* is Peirce's dualistic metaphysics of that which we know of and that which is beyond the limit of ordinary concept of knowing.

The concept of *Tao* also is divided into two. The first concept of *Tao* is that we know and the second concept of *Tao* is something beyond our ordinary knowledge. I will first lay out different explanations upon *Tao* and then concentrate on Lao Tzu's concept of *Tao* in comparison with Peirce's cosmology. First here is what ordinary Chinese think about *Tao*. Kim, Yong Jeong writes:

> The term Tao, that Chinese people whether Taoists or Confucianists are fond of using, means process of the

universe, the order of nature, Tao of human and the of society. Therefore, Chinese thought is centered in functional and relational propositions which are according to active transaction between yin and yang polarities.[75]

In a sense, *Tao* is the way of the universe, and what people believe as the order of nature. It is important that the concept of *Tao* is within the culture of Chinese life. As Raju sees it that the biggest gorge in understanding of *Tao* resides in between Confucianism and Taoism. Raju makes a clearly visible comparison. Raju writes about confucian *Tao* as:

> The idea of Tao is common to all philosophers in China, though each school interprets it in its own way. For Confucius, The Tao has nothing mystical about it. It is not an entity, not a substantial thing. It is only a way of conduct, leading to the happiness of all mankind, and changing according to circumstances.[76]

In this regard of Confucian *Tao*, it is a way of conduct or may be put simply 'way'. *Tao* is humanly way to follow to gain

---

75) Kim, Yong Jeong, *The Third Tide of Philosophy,* Bum Yang Sa, 1998, p. 409.

76) P. T. Raju, *Introduction to Comparative Philosophy,* University of Nebraska Press, 1962, p. 109.

happiness. It is the way that one has to choose in his conduct within the changing state of circumstance. This concept of *Tao* of man described by Confucius is not compatible with the eternal, everlasting *Tao* of Taoism. Raju goes on writes about Taoist *Tao* as:

> The Tao is the Absolute of the Taoists. It is the Way in man. It was made a thing and given metaphysical significance. It is spontaneity itself. It has no purpose and motive. It is both Being and Non-being; both issue from the Tao. Tao is power inherent in a thing and constitutes its nature and law and is the universe.... ....It is the nature of the Tao to jump from one extreme to its opposite. Being becomes Non-being and Non-being becomes Being.[77]

Even thought, there is certain logic in constituting Lao Tzu's theory of *Tao*, but there is a line drew upon the theory of *Tao* beyond which theory is conveyed meta-logically. If *Tao* is of such nature, how would one live according to Non-being? Compared to Confucian *Tao*, Taoist's *Tao* is not entirely humanly. Now, Let us focus on Lao Tzu's *Tao* In *Tao-te Ching*. *Tao-te Ching* opens as follows:

---

77) Ibid., p. 122.

> “道可道 非常道, 名可名 非常名, 無名天地之始 有名萬物之母.”
>
> "The Tao(Way) that can be told of is not the eternal Tao; The name that can be named is not the eternal name. The Nameless is the origin of Heaven and Earth; The Names is the mother of all things."[78]

There are many interpretations upon these lines of *Tao-te Ching*. In *Tao-te Ching*, the opening line says "it can not be told or named", but is silly that many tries to put it in a word or sentence to explicate what it is. We may look at several of them selected by Alan Watts:

> -The Tao that can be told of is not the Absolute Tao(Lin Yutang).
> -The Way that can be told is not an Unvarying Way(Waley).
> -The Tao that is the subject of discussion is not the true Tao(Old).
> -The Way that may truly be regarded as the way is other than a permanent way(Duyvendak).
> -The Flow that can be followed is not the eternal flow(Aunt).
> -The course that can be discoursed is not the eternal Course(Aunt).
> -The force that is forced is not true Force(Aunt).

78) Wing-Tsit Chan, *Chinese Philosophy,* Princeton Univ. Press, 1973, p. 139.

-The Tao that can be tao-ed is not the invariable Tao(Fung Yu-lan, [Bodde]).[79)]

As we can see above we have various translation on the concept of *Tao*. Different terms are displayed; absolute *Tao*, Unvarying way, true *Tao*, permanent way, eternal flow, true force, etc... Let me borrow explanation from Peirce about his Tychism; "...it is true nature of the universe and can not be explained away" Among the many terms explaining *Tao* let me choose 'true *Tao*' for the convenience of the argument. It seems to me Lao Tzu wanted the true *Tao* to be something not exploited and explained away. Here, I give one vote to Peirce's expression. But if we are to pull out a common thing for the sake of argument, it would be such that Lao Tzu has two-fold concepts of *Tao*. There is mundane *Tao* which can be told or named and there is eternal *Tao* which is absolute or true. The former is not quite diversified with Confucian *Tao* and the latter seems the true *Tao* that Lao Tzu stresses. What we can tell or name can be taken as knowable. Lao Tzu says of this former *Tao* the mother of all things. But on the other hand, the nameless is the origin of Heaven an Earth. Lao Tzu seems to put priority on the latter eternal *Tao*. I would like to put the difference

79) Alan Watts, *Tao: The Water Course Way*, Pelican Books, 1981, p. 39.

between *Tao* and *Ch'ang Tao*(常道) as growing up and growing old. Growing up and growing old have, in a way, different concept, but again both can be taken as one. There is no naturally drawn line between growing up and growing old. It seems clear that Lao Tzu's concept of *Tao* is nothing like western dualism. There seems of no strict dividing line in between the two. If we interpret, in western way, *Tao* as 'principle of the world', that *Tao* must be the eternal *Tao*; *Ch'ang Tao*(常道). Alan Watts interprets as; the true, eternal and authentic *Tao* that is not fixed. Thus Watts writes:

> From strictly logical point of view, this means nothing and gives us no information. Tao is just a name for whatever happens, or, as Lao Tzu put it. "The Tao principle is what happens of it-self(tzu-jan 自然).[80]

True, eternal *Tao* is *Ch'ang Tao*(常道) and it can not be told or named. When we perceive nature and life we gain perception upon mundane *Tao*. The eternal *Tao* is not our ordinary object of sensory perception. There are two more lines that we need to look:

> That which has no name" and "that which has a name"

80) Ibid., p. 38.

> are explained elsewhere in the text in this fashion: "something is born of nothing." Once the world begins existing it becomes the Mother.[81)]

> It is the nature of the Tao to jump from one extreme to its opposite. Being becomes Non-being and Non-being becomes Being[82)]

'Named *Tao* is mother of all thing' means that it corresponds the mundane humanly business of the world so that we can attain sensory perception to have knowledge. But it is not true *Tao*. Lao Tzu seems to constantly stress of nameless true *Tao*. As stated above by Raju, true *Tao* is becoming non-being from being and being from non-being. This is certainly not a earthly humanly concept.

Being from non-being is not a physically possible phenomenon. I suggest that what we call physical and attain 'certainty' from it may be the only little portion of the whole story of the universe. This is the idea of Peirce discussed above. At this poind let us recall Peirce's idea of Tychism: absolute chance or event without causal antecedent. Peirce says that the

---

81) Man-jan Cheng, *Lao-Tzu "My words are very easy to understand,"* trans. by Tam C. Gibbs, North Atlantic Books, 1981, p. 20.

82) P. T. Raju, *Introduction to Comparative Philosophy,* University of Nebraska Press, 1962, p. 122.

novelty of Tychism is the true nature of universe. Most important of all is that the novelty can not be explained away.

One thing is clear that Lao Tzu has dual aspects of *Tao*. If we take *Tao* as 'way' or 'the principle of the world', it would not be entirely misleading that Lao Tzu has dual aspects on the world; one aspect of the world is mundane humanly parameter and other is truly authentic self moving in fluctuating world. Of the many explanations above on true *Tao*, I would like to make an alinement between Peirce and Lao Tzu. As we have seen above that Peirce holds on to both Tychism; new chance, and Synechism; habit-taking continuity. Both chance and continuity are necessary factors for evolution.

Without evolution which truly means changes, the universe can not be in a system of organismically fluctuating body of mass. We see here a great similarity between Lao Tzu's and Peirce's cosmology. As a scientist educated in the west, Peirce has different look onto the world. It is not an outcome of western scientific discovery. It is Peirce's extra-conventional cosmology and metaphysics. It is interestingly close to Chinese traditional thoughts, but it is not sure that it is Chinese influence. On this organismic view on the universe, Peirce, as a scientist, in his system of Tychism, can afford indeterministic plasticity of mind or any other indeterministic set up of the world.

Both Peirce and Lao Tzu talk about dual aspects of the world. It is their cosmology and epistemology. In space, time and state, the world is fluctuating. Peirce has to have both 'continuity' and 'emergence' in his system to afford an evolving kind of world. Synechism stands for 'continuity' that we can know about and Tychism stands for 'emergence' that we can not know about. This is Peirce's system of Tychism/Synechism. It does not matter how the terminologies look.

For the same matter, if we look at the matter in pure epistemologial stance, Lao Tzu differentiates the world into '*Tao*' of two kinds: '*Tao*' of mundane world and '*Tao*' beyond such world. The former '*Tao*' is what we can conceive through sensory perception and the latter is not conceivable through sensory perception. If we would give a match between Peirce and Lao Tzu, Synechism will go in to the former '*Tao*' and Tychism will go in to the latter '*Tao*'. In both system, there are two sides in the cosmology about what we can normally know and about what we can not.

In his system of Tychism/Synechism, Peirce disavows the traditional western epistemology that says "…to know about things all the way…." For Peirce, the universe is too big and wild to know its true character, and that is Tychism. It is about knowing and so is Lao Tzu's '*Tao*'. Even though their footings and contents are not perfectly identical, Tychism/Synechism and the '*Ch'ang 'Tao'*/'*Tao*' can be construed in parallel alinements in between the two system.

- Epistemology: Dewey and Chuang Tzu -

In the matter of knowing, traditional western philosophy divides subjects from objects, and subjects inquire objects to be analyzed deductively. This way of analytic deduction renders causal reductionism, so that, the world is taken to be composite of atoms that can provide generalized understanding of the world. In chapter 2 section 3 above, I have argued that one of the problems in western epistemology is epistemic stance of dichotomy that perception is outcome by strict division of subject and object. Traditional western legacy of knowing is criticized by Dewey as 'spectator theory.' Dewey writes:

> There was bequeathed to generation of thinkers in intrinsically a more beholding of viewing of reality-the spectator conception of knowledge.[83]

83) John Dewey, *Reconstruction in Philosophy*, The Beacon Press, 1963, p. 112.

When subject of knowing is taken as spectator, object can be free from subject-matter and become truly objectified. Here, in this section, I will present Dewey's and Chuang Tzu's epistemology that conceive subject and objects in course of knowing inseparably. In this system of monistic epistemology, where subjects are within the commingled state of ever changing world, nothing is static, thus, causal reduction is limited. Both subjects and objects are in state of constant interaction.

In Chinese philosophy, presentation of real world before us does not render knowledge of the external world. Inner experience of immediate intuition is what truly counts in Chinese epistemology. In western philosophy we perceive external world, while, in Chinese philosophy, we are the objects. Unlike traditional western philosophy, Dewey gives weight on subjectivity in epistemology. In this section, I will argue western attitude to pursue fixed right answer to the world is due to subject/object dichotomy. The first step in Dewey's system is to give up on the concept of unchanging right answers of the world. Dewey writes:

> From its simplest to its most far-reaching activities it holds itself open to revision in a degree made strikingly clear by

what happened to the Newtonian account of gravitation after its quarter millennium of established 'certainty'. The more scientific and accurate observation becomes, the less does it claim ultimacy for the specific assertions it achieves.[84)]

Dewey discharges the concept of certainty in his epistemology. Newtonian laws of physical mechanism is held responsible for the generally taken attitude in knowing. Dewey is arguing such tradition in epistemology no more binding in metaphysics and science. Dewey's criticism on traditional western epistemology and Dewey's own account of knowing goes on. And then Chuang Tzu's monistic epistemology will be presented to be compared with Dewey's system of knowing. For general character of eastern and western epistemology Kim, Yong Jeong writes as follows:

through theory processes and patterns of thoughts, we can tell that, in the east it is stressed that knowing is directed to *comprehensiveness of unification* and differentiation, whereas in the west, it is stressed that knowing is toward *division and analysis* of compound bodies.[85)]

---

84) John Dewey and Arthur F. Bentley, *Knowing and the Known,* Beacon Press, 1960, p. 79.

85) Kim, Yong Jeong , *The Third Tide of Philosophy,* Bum Yang Sa, 1997, p.

My goal in this part of the chapter is to show unification of subject and object in Dewey's and Chuang Tzu's accounts of knowing. For Dewey knowledge is a part of experience. When we divide the world into separate objects, we undergo classifying and analyzing. Dewey argues that knowledge seems to break up reality, and objectifying of perceived objects is a necessary step in perception. However, Dewey argues that pure division between subject and object is not possible.

> We proceed upon the postulate that knowings are always and everywhere inseparable from the knowns - that the two are twin aspects of common fact.[86]

Experience is the most important affair in knowing. Experience for Dewey is continuous transaction between human beings and their environing states. For Dewey, the major means of experience is observation. Let us take a look at what Dewey has to say about transactional observation:

> Transactional observation is the fruit of an insistence upon the right to proceed in freedom to select and view all

---

409.

86) John Dewey and Arthur F. Bentley, *Knowing and the Known,* Beacon Press, 1960, p. 53.

> subject-matters in whatever way seems desirable under reasonable hypothesis, and regardless of ancient claims on behalf of either minds or material mechanism, or any of the surrogates of either.[87]

Experience is the organic connection of living human beings and their natural and artificial environment. Organic and continuous relation is the key concept in process of knowing. Human beings are not absolute 'individual' or 'subject' who bridge between a human being and other human beings and other things of nature. As it is discussed above, Newtonian laws of physical mechanism was held responsible for traditional epistemic attitude. Dewey, however, employs one of Newton's law of physics in delivering his account of knowing.

> Where the older approach had most commonly seen self-action in "the facts", the newer approach took form under Newton as a interaction, marked especially by the third "law of motion"- that action and reaction are equal and opposite.[88]

In Dewey's system, in the relation between subject/object

---

87) Ibid., p. 124.

88) Ibid., p. 68.

and knower/known, there is no room for individuation. It is like the motion of pendulum. In this respect, all motions are related. One motion causes opposite motion and since all are co-related, motion-causing-motions are continuous. Dewey puts traditional view of 'self-action' an older approach. Human beings are originally attached to other human beings and surrounding natural environment. The relation is continuous and organismic. Continuity here means the opposite of temporality.

Human beings are natural organism themselves and always in states of organismic relation with their environment. In this organismic states that are evolving along with time and environment, we the organismic bodies, develop intelligence. According to Dewey, intelligence is not an innate given. Dewey criticizes traditional view as follows:

> ....When they maintain the traditional philosophy of intellectualism- that is, of knowing as something self-sufficing and self enclosed.[89]

It is humanly developed habit of inquiry, reflection, adapting to the environment, solving of problem and most of all

89) John Dewey, *Reconstruction in Philosophy*, The Beacon Press, 1963, p. 117.

overcoming various characters and their unstable changes. Intelligence is on-going of adaptation and tools for refining our transaction and interaction with the environing states. In this organismic relation of human beings and the nature, intelligence of any live subjects is in the direction of improvement.

Dewey calls himself a radical empiricist. Like Peirce argues above in chapter 3 section 1, Dewey does not believe or accept the concept of 'soul'. As we have seen in chapter 3 section 2 that Dewey is a biological monist. Human beings are organismic bodies and intelligence emerges at a certain point in keeping organism growth. Dewey does not take anything 'supersensible' or 'supernatural'. Dewey opposes the metaphysical concept of state reality that traditional philosophy calls 'substance'. For Dewey things of this world are not static and all there is constant changing and interacting each other. Human beings are not 'absolute individual' as subjects.

Everyone has different angle of vision. Experience includes experiencer, experienced and the way of experiencing. Therefore always there is privacy in each experience as well as common ground. Experience is an individual process, thus, privacy of experience is the necessity for the phenomena. However, there is communication of each individual, so that, social common ground is also a basis of individuality. Dewey argues that there is no such a thing as a 'pure' individuality. Each human being is in the intersection within many factors. An experience is 'mine' because I am included in it. But the subjectivity of my own perception is not all there is in experience. Kim, Dong Shik interprets Dewey's account of experience in such a way that knowing as one eating food. When one eats something, there is change in one's metabolism and there is also change in something that is eaten. Kim, Dong Shik writes:

> Through eating, both an organism and the environment undergo certain changes. Likewise, through action of knowing both the knower and the known are changed. For Dewey, the strict epistemic dichotomy of subject/object is due to wrong footed theory based on inadequate old psychology.[90]

When 'I' experiences, beautiful flowers on the street, Dewey argues that I, the subject of experience develops the pleasantness. Whatever the feeling is from the situation, the outcome of my pleasant experience is a result of that very

90) Kim, Dong Shik, 金東植, *Dewey's Instrumentalism and Rorty's Neopragmatism,* Hwarangdae Research Institute, 2001, p. 12.

surrounding states. My experience is an outcome of the whole environing situation. The pleasantness is inspired by the flower and everything else in the surrounding circumstance. And 'I' feel that feeling 'I' am changed along with everything else in that situation including the flowers.

Unlike Lockean one-way relation of knowing, this is a two-way relation. Simply stated, my perception also give an affect on what is perceived. Dewey stresses on this holistic procedure of experience. There is no sole individuality as a subject of knowing. Every factor including subject itself is interwoven in experience.

In comparison between Dewey and Chinese epistemology, we can focus on subject and object relation. The major theme of this book is, after all, to repudiate the western epistemic attitude of subject/object dichotomy. As we have seen above Dewey's epistemology, knower and known are not entirely separated. This implies subject-matter is included in knowing process. We can see this kind of epistemological attitude in Chinese philosophy. I will open the argument with James K. Fiebleman's interpretation on Lao Tzu's account of knowledge:

> The most subtle knowledge is not rational but intuitive and unconscious, a matter of feeling. As often as not taste

makes judgements better than reasoning can. The taoists advocate this kind of knowledge over the kind that is deliberate and rational. The practices of one who known in this way are apt to be more relaxed as well as a accurate.[91)]

As we can see above, most subtle knowledge is not rational but intuitive. This can be considered as a maxim in Taoist epistemology. Intuitive acknowledgement is unconscious spontaneous matter of feeling. This is interesting to notice that in western traditional system rationality is the main tool constituting knowing and knowledge. When rationality is the basic language in knowledge, a base is secured where individual disputes can not take places. Intuition on the other hand does not afford a firmer ground for everyone. An old Greek saying that man are the measure of all thing is not our immediate interest at the moment. Our interest is how Chinese developed civilized culture under different epistemic attitude. My goal in this section is to show common ground between Dewey and Chuang Tzu.

The procedure of knowing is practiced over a long period of time and become automatic and not to require conscious

91) James K. Fiebleman, *Understanding Oriental Philosophy,* New American Library, 1976, p. 110.

deliberation.

T'ang Chűn-i shortly analyses Chinese epistemology as follows:

> I shall limit this paper to the four important typical ways thinking about the individual and the world in chinese epistemology.
>
> 1. To think of the individual as objectively existing as a part of world.
> 2. To think of the world as a part of, or the content of, oridentical with the being of the individual subject.
> 3. To think that both the individual and the world must transcended and that there is then a reality neither individual nor world.
> 4. To think that both the individual subject and the object world are to be asserted positively as existing. Yet neither is asserted as a part of, or the content of, or identical with, the other, nor are they asserted as mutually exclusive, because their mutual transcendence and mutual immanence are both accepted.[92)]

As we can see from the above passages, the basic format in Chinese epistemology is the mutuality between individual subject and object world. There is no sharp line dividing in

92) T'ang Chűn-i, "The Individual and the World in Chinese Methodology," *The Chinese Mind*, ed. by Charles. A. Moore, University Press of Hawaii, 1977, p. 265.

the two. The reality is, in short, individuality is in the world as well as the objects in that contents of the world.

Fung Yu-Lan also write about world objects in term of *Tao* as follows:

> …Thus it is that there are roof-slate and pillars, ugliness and beauty, the peculiar and the extraordinary. All these by means of the *Tao* and united and become one. …Although all things differ, they are alike in that they all constitute something and are good for something. They all equally come from the *Tao*. Therefor from the view point of the *Tao*, things, though different, yet are united and become one.[93)]

Fung Yu-Lan goes on explain Chuang Tzu's cosmology and epistemology in terms of unity:

> The universe is the unity of all things. If we attain this unity and identity ourselves with it, then the members of our body are but so much dust and dirt, while life and death, and beginning, are but as the succession of day and night, which cannot disturb our inner peace. How much less shall we be troubled by worldly gain and loss. Good-luck and bad-luck(ch 20). Thus Chuang Tzu solved the original

93) Fung Yu-Lan, *History of Chinese Philosophy,* The Free Press, 1966, p. 112.

problem of Taoists simply by abolishing it. This really the philosophical way of solving problems.[94)]

Abolishing here would not mean giving up of the entire world object. Something is to abolish and something is not. The line between the two are like the line between the bright side the moon and the dark side the moon. We can observe the bright side the moon the we should just leave off the dark-side the moon for now. Chuang Tzu draws a line in between humanly earthly part and the part beyond that. James R. Ware interprets Chuang Tzu's concept of *liu-he-chih-nei* 六合之內 and *liu-he-chih-wai* 六合之外. 六合之內 is our immediate interest of the world of *t'ien hsia* 天·下, and *tung-hsi-nan-bei* 東·西·南·北, in mundane earthly world of our every day life. And the other, 六合之外 is the world above and beyond that, so that, Chuang Tzu puts it in parentheses for the time being. James R. Ware translate it as:

> We conclude therefore, that in every analysis there is something unanalyzable; in every argument, there is something not subject to argument. If you are still in doubt, I can only that the sage cherishes the topic in his bosom(the knows intuitively)······ Knowledge is at its peak when it

---

94) Ibid., p. 115.

> stops with what it does not know, who really understands the argument that uses no words, or the utterance that does no articulating? Anybody who does understand shall be called nature's depot, to be poured into without ever becoming full or poured from without ever becoming full or poured from without becoming dry and without the source of capacity.[95]

According to Ware, *Chuang tzu* says of "*tao-t'ung-wei-i* 道通爲一". Innate "*kwang-ming-chih-hui* 光明智慧" attains *Tao* "*ch'üeh-te* 覺得": I and *Tao* are not two but become one.[96] Everything is in *Tao* become one. In Chinese philosophy, dichotomy of subject/object may give clearness of perception but it divides human and nature in two, then sensory experience blocks intuitive mental activity ,thus, there rises side-effect of diversifying reaction. Wing-Tsit Chan writes:

> The true man, according to Chuang Tzu , is he who comprehends and lives in the underlying of the Tao. He has achieved a happiness that is beyond all change, a life that is beyond life and death.[97]

---

95) James R. Ware, *The Saying of Chuang-tzu.* A New Translation Confucius Publishing Co. 1959, p. 22.

96) James R. Ware, "Introduction," *The Saying of Chuang-tzu.* A new translation, Confucius Publishing Co., 1959.

97) Wing-Tsit Chan, *Sources of Chinese Tradition,* Vol. 1, compiled by William

The difficulty of forming a standard of knowing is that subject–matter is involved in epistemology(Some say mystic part of Chuang Tzu). But here in this context, we are interested in Chuang Tzu's epistemology of the mundane world that we become one that experiencing changes constantly. That seems to have concrete common ground with Dewey's epistemology. Wing–Tsit Chan writes:

> The pure man makes this oneness his eternal abode, in which he becomes a "companion" of Nature and does not attempt to interfere with it by imposing the way man on it.[98)]

Thus in Chinese epistemology especially in Taoism epistemology knowing is a process to combine the knower and the known. Thomé H. Fang writes:

> Nature and human nature are two in one, giving form to what I have called the comprehensive harmony, a harmony between ingrowing parts as well as a harmony with surrounding. In this form of primordial unity, all that seems various and antipathetic is to intrinsically related

---

Theodore de Bary, Burton Watson. Columbia Univ. Press, 1960, p. 63.

98) Wing–Tsit Chan, *Chinese Philosophy,* Princeton University Press, 1973, p. 177.

that it strikes together sympathetic chords to the accompaniment of song of love, which is an encomium of life.[99]

Let me organize those sayings about Chuang Tzu in terms of Dewey's account. It can be put in three headings. First, as Heracleitos said, the world is constantly changing. Both Dewey and Chuang Tzu agree on this and they believe we are within the change ourselves. And second, Chuang Tzu has understanding of dual aspects of the world. Here, Chuang Tzu draw a line between mundane humanly conceivable world and the world beyond that. And third, of knowing, there is becoming oneness of both knower and known. Wing-Tsit Chan calls it "oneness", and Thomé H. Fang calls it "comprehensive harmony." This view is seemingly recognized in Dewey's system of epistemology. We might consider both theories as 'holistic epistemology of monism'.

99) Thomé H. Fang, "Chinese Wisdom," *Chinese Philosophy,* Vol. 1, China Academy, 1974, p. 297.

Chapter 6. Conclusion;
A new Paradigm Proposed from the Vintages

In this book, various disciplines of eastern and western philosophy were discussed. At a first glance, it might seem as mere comparison between philosophy of mind of the East and the West or a presentation of Chinese epistemology and Peirce's Dewey's philosophical system. But, as a matter of fact, I intentionally brought out the problem of mind on the table of discussion to show that the philosophy of mind or cognitive science in western philosophy should be re-examined for their epistemological attitude that hold on to the law of causality and deterministic view on the world. It is in fact a habitual attitude of western philosophy that has been mainly based on the epistemological dichotomy that takes 'the world' and 'I' separately. And they understand things in the world are composites of more static atomic makes-up of smaller particles. In the West, they generally take that the smaller it gets more static and individualistic it gets, which guarantees firmer and certain facts about things in the nature. This can be called an

Atomistic legacy of western science and philosophy as well. In western analytic philosophy, they understand the physical concept of matters as collision and combination of granular composites. Pendulum of balls is a good example of Newtonian system, but this idea of pendulum was ironically used by Dewey, as illustrated in Chapter 2 section3 above, in refuting traditional western metaphysical system. However, it is, after all, true that the traditional western system of law of causality has been the motoring power in western civilization, especially in natural science. However, my goal was to show that the law of causality is not the only way of understanding the nature. This gives a cue point for our discussion. The Chinese philosophy and Peirce and Dewey have different views about the world; about the world that constantly fluctuates, we only know only part of it, nothing is static and purely individual. Thus, they accept it that we have our limit of knowing of the world.

The first half of this book was to see the problem of philosophy of mind would meet the problem of causality, and the second half of this book was to re-appreciate various Chinese approaches and Peirce's and Dewey's account of mind. In chapter 2 section 3, I argued that the problem resides not in methodology but in epistemology and metaphysics. Thus,

I had to focus on epistemology and metaphysics on the half of this book to refute the law of causality in dealing with organic feature of mind. I argue that it might be worthwhile to scan around different region of philosophy in the world.

We should keep that in mind that the holding on and going on with the law of causality and deterministic approach are refutable. The habit-taking natures of the world were taken and understood in the form of cause and effect chain. This way, features of natural phenomena were taken, collected, and employed as data of science. In this course, science has been achieving great development. And this has been shown its fruitful result in most field of natural science. Then, I wonder how the old Chinese thinkers such as Confucius, Mencius, Lao Tzu or Chuang Tzu would have said about their cosmology if they had current up-dated knowledge about the universe and the scientific discoveries that we have now. This can be an interesting question. However, on the other hand, from the late 19th century, our view upon the world in science started to be taken differently. The law of causality and determinism started to be taken differently from "the right answer" for this universe. Starting with Peirce to the era of Prigogine, theories of indeterminacy, chaos and evolutionary view on the universe were sprouted. And thus, in modern times, our cosmology is quite apart from that of Newtonian version. Some of modern science has changed its attitude in epistemology. I argue that philosophy of mind should have altered its method of approach long ago as modern physics did. This is the reason I brought out philosophy of mind on the table of discussion at the first place.

In chapter 2 section 1 and section 2, I briefly presented passages of western philosophy of mind. I talked about functionalism and its main problem of multiple realization which leads the whole matter of cognitive science to the direction of physical simulation of brain work. In western philosophy, the relation of mind and body was taken in the name of behaviorism which was based on cause and effect relation of physics and mentality. In this method extra-causal feature of mind is inexplicable. This problem was discussed in the problem of qualia and intentionality. This can be called in other word, 'organismic features of mind'. To overcome this problem the idea of P.D.P or connectionism were discussed, but these too, cannot escape from the closedness of causality and determinism, which means organismic feature of mind still can not be solved. In one word, it can be called as 'plasticity of mind'. There is no strict rule that a certain input of bodily physical cause will result mental output as effect in general accordance. How an input will result an certain output in mental reaction can not be explained in the cause and effect law of physics. Organismic character of mind includes pattern recognition, active correction of distorted input, rehabilitative reaction for injured system, adaptation through generalizing the received knowledge...etc. In chapter 2 section 3, I tried to show that the problem of western philosophy of mind is due to their ground of approach: the closedness of causality and deterministic treat of mind. Thus, I argued that problem of talking about mind should descend to epistemological attitude. For this reason, I provided the shifting of scientific attitude. For example, I talked Prigogine's law of entropy and the views of pluralistic universe. All that saying were to refute the idea of "right answers for the static universe". Epistemology is formed on top of metaphysics and cosmology. Therefore, about one third of this book dealt with differently grounded epistemology that were about Chinese approach and Peirce's and Dewey's system of knowing.

Chapter 3 was about somewhat different approach of Dewey's account of mind, to elucidate their position, we need to employ terms like "evolutionary cosmology", "different kind of monism" or "emergent theory." Dewey takes the problem of mind as matter of science, so that they reject any religious concepts upon mind or supernatural ideas upon mind. They too employ the method of material reduction and thus reached to the idea that mind's acts are natural phenomena. But, the important point here is that their reduction process ends at the level of biology. In their theories at a certain point of physical development, 'emergence' of mentality suddenly takes place on top of physical base. In traditional western view emergence means any occurrence without a causal antecedence. This kind of argument can only be taken as a scientific mystery in western scientific point of view. The main goal to study their theories on mind is to see how scientifically oriented philosopher such as Dewey could rest on such unscientific endings. To discuss this we have to descend to the matter of epistemology and metaphysics, and these were discussed in chapter 5.

Chapter 4 dealt with various Chinese thoughts on mind. My intention here was to show the compatibility between Chinese thoughts and Peirce's and Dewey's accounts on mind and the diversity with traditional and modern cognitive science, and then it was discussed that the footing of Chinese thoughts on mind were sensibility related to the traditional Chinese metaphysics and epistemology that accepts wilderness of the nature and acceptance of our limit in conceiving them for such a time being. Chinese thoughts on mind are, to begin with, not based on mind/body dualism such as of the West. But it is interesting that we can find similar monistic kind of concept from western culture such as a famous popular song's lyric that says "...listen to your heart...". We need to pay an attention to the point that both Chinese thoughts on mind, and Peirce's and Dewey's account can rest on such, in western scientific point of view, mystic progress and conclusion. We need to look into their difference in epistemological and metaphysical ground to understand this matter. The discussion upon this matter was passed on to next chapter.

In chapter 5, Peirce's system of epistemology was brought out and compared with Chinese thoughts especially Lao Tzu's dual aspects of *Tao*. Peirce argues that what we know and take as a truth is not a truth but only opinion. And there are two sides of the world: the world that we can know and the world that we can not know. This cosmology of Peirce was compared with Lao Tzu's dual aspects of *Tao* and *Ch'ang Tao*. And, Dewey's idea of 'I' and 'the 'world' are not two but one, that interact each other in knowing, was compared with Chuang Tzu's epistemology of 'comprehensive harmony' or 'oneness'. They were arranged in parallel structure for the convenience of comparison; comparison that were to show their similarity. On this different metaphysical scheme of indeterminism, the attitude of taking unknown or not being able to grab a unchanging answer as mystery of the world. Chinese philosophy seem to rest on their traditional epistemology.

The relation and common domain of Bergson's "Philosophy of living", Peirce's, James' and Dewey's "Organismic Philosophy" are understandable because they are all contemporaries and known for their close communication. However, there is one thing that I could not go on discussing. That is to investigate the cause and progression that how early American philosophy such as pragmatism of Peirce and Dewey could share similar ground of world view with old Chinese philosophy. It remains as an interesting question for the time being.

Philosophy of mind or rather cognitive science is now in two line up, one that pursues material reduction of mind into other physical means, and the other that keeps refuting the idea of brain simulation on the base of anti-reductionism. Both seem not quite successful in what they are doing. This does not make any progress in understanding mind or mental act. We should notice that even the anti-reductionists are doing their work on the base materialism and analytic trend of western philosophy. In criticizing western analytic trend, in his book *Philosophy and the Mirror of Nature*, Rorty says that what they were saying are the same stories after all.

The theme of this book is not about a discussion on western philosophy of mind. The reason that western philosophy of mind was brought out on the table of discussion was to start out with the derived problem of closedness of causality. And it is taken as problem of epistemology and metaphysics in this book. I propose it now that it is a time to look back the vintages from our passage from in and out of our institutionalized system of western way of understanding the world. I am not arguing that the vintage from Chinese philosophy or other side-steamer systems are the right ones. There is no ready made right answer. But if we take up a moment to see the outside the wall of current paradigm, we may get a new idea for a 'new age of philosophy'. It is a trial of a cross-over of between different disciplines proposing a determinism to give an allowance of a little room for what they call "mystic."

Glossary of Chinese Names

Ch'eng I	程頤
Chuang Tzu	莊子
Chu Hsi	朱熹
Confucius	孔子
Confucianism	儒敎
ching-ch'i	精氣
ching-ch'un	精純
ching-shen	精神
Chou Tun-i	周敦頤
ching-shen-chŭ-hsing-t'i	精神居形體
Fung yu-lan	馮友蘭
Fan zhen	范縝
Huan T'an	桓譚
hsing-hsian-chin-hsi-hsiang-wuan	性相近 習相遠
hsing-chŭ-erh-shen-sheng	形具而神生

Hsün Tzu	荀子
I Ching	易經
chüeh-te	覺得
kwang-ming-chih-hui	光明智慧
Lao Tzu	老子
li/ch'i	理/氣
Lin Yü-t'ang	林語堂
Lü-shih ch'un-ch'iu	呂氏春秋
Lu-Wang	陸王
Man-jan Cheng	鄭曼髯
Mencius	孟子
liu-he-chih-nei	六合之內
liu-he-chih-wai	六合之外
Lun-yü	論語
Liu Shu-hsien	劉述先
t'ai-chi	太極
t'ai-chi-t'u	太極圖
Tao/Ch'ang Tao	道/常道
Tao-te Ching	道德經
Taoism	道家
tao-t'ung-wei-i	道通爲一

T'ang Chün-i	唐君毅
T'ien-lun	天論
t'ien-hsia	天下
tung-hsi-nan-bei	東西南北
Thomé H. Fang	方東美
tzu-jan	自然
Wei Tat	韋達
Huang Wen-shan	黃文山
Wing-Tsit Chan	陳榮捷
wu-chi	無極
yin - yang	陰 - 陽

Bibliography

- Alexander, S., *Space Time, and Deity*, Dover Publication, inc. New York, 1920.

- Block, Ned J. and Fodor, Jerry, "What Psychological State are not," *The Philosophical Review*, Vol. 81, Cornell Univ., 1972.

- Burwood, Stephen, *Philosophy of Mind,*, University of Hull, UCL. Press, 1998.

- Dennet, Daniel, "Intentional System," *The Journal of Philosophy*, Vol. 68, 1971.

- Cheng, Man-Jan, Lao-tzu, "*My words are very easy to understand*," trans. by Tam C. Gibbs, North Atlantic Books, 1981.

- Chan, Wing-Tsit, *Sources of Chinese Tradition Vol.,1*, Compiled by William, Theodore De Bary, Burton Watson, Columbia Univ. Press, New York, 1960.

- Chan, Wing-Tsit, *Chinese Philosophy*, Princeton Univ. Press, 1973.

- Dewey, John, *Experience and nature,* Open Court Publishing Co., 1926.

- Dewey, John, *On Experience, Nature , and Freedom,* The Bobbs-Merrill Co. Inc., 1960.

- Dewey, John, *Reconstruction in Philosophy*, The Beacon Press, Boston, 1963.

- Dewey, John and Arthur F. Bentley, *Knowing and the Known,* Beacon Press, Boston, 1960.

- Dewey, John, *Intelligence in the Modern World,* The Modern Library, New York, 1939.

- Fang, Thomé H., "Chinese Wisdom," *Chinese Philosophy,* Vol. 1, China Academy, 1974.

- Fiebleman, James K., *Understanding Oriental Philosophy*, New American Library, 1976.

- Fung, Yu-Lan, *History of Chinese Philosophy,* The Free Press, New York, 1966.

- Heil, John, *Philosophy of Mind,* Routledge, 1998.

- http://www.jracademy.com/~jtucek/science/what.html.

- Huang, Wen-Shan, "T'ai Chi Ch'uan and I-Ching, or the book of the Changes," *Chinese Philosophy,* Vol. 1, China Academy, 1974.

- James, William, *Pragmatism,* Logman's Green, New York, 1907.

- Kim, Choong-Yeol, 金忠烈, "Thoughts of Philosophy in the Chin Period," *Research of the Lü-shih ch'un-ch'iu*, Taiwan Univ., 1987.

- Kim, Choong-Yeol, "Introduction to Chinese Human nature," *Theory of Substance and Human Nature in Chinese Philosophy,* Yeon Sei Univ. Press, 1982.

- Kim, Dong-Shik, 金東植, *Dewey's Instrumentalism and Rorty's*

Neopragmatism, Hwarangdae Research Institute, 2001.

- Kim, Jae-Gwon, *Philosophy of Mind,* West View Press, 1996.

- Kim, Sang-Il, 金相日, *Whitehead and Eastern Philosophy*, Seo Guang Sa, 1993.

- Kim, Yeong-Jung, 金泳楨, *Philosophy of Mind and Cognitive Science,* Philosophy and Current Matters Co., 1996.

- Kim, Yong Jeong, 金鎔貞, "Entropy and Prigogine's Dissipative Structure," *Science Philosophy and Culture,* Bum Yang Sa, 1996.

- Kim, Yong-Jeong, "The Dissolution of a Material Substance and the Description by Space or Field," *Philosophy and Science,* Bum Yang Sa, 1997.

- Kim, Yong-Jeong, *The Third Tide of Philosophy,* Bum Yang Sa, 1998.

- Liu, Shu-Hsien, "The Function of the Mind in Chu Hsi's Philosophy," *Journal of Chinese Philosophy 5,* by D. Reidel Publishing Co., 1978.

- Mcginn, Colin, *Mind and Bodies,* Oxford Univ. Press, 1997.

- *McGraw-Hill Encyclopedia of Physics*, Sydil P. Paker & McGraw-Hill Inc., 1981.

- Murray G. Murphey, *The Development of Peirce's Philosophy*, Hackett Publishing Co. Inc., 1961.

- *Philosophy of John Dewey*, Evanston and Chicago, 1939.

- *Collected Papers of Charles Sanders Peirce,* The Belknap Press of Harvard Univ. Press, 1965.

- Putam, Hillary, "Mind, Language and Reality," *Philosophical Paper,* Vol. II, Cambridge, 1975.

- Raju, P. T., *Introduction to Comparative Philosophy*, University of Nevbraska Press, 1962.

- Rorty, Richard, *Philosophy and the Mirror of Nature,* Princeton University Press, 1980.

- Ryle, Gilbert, *The Concept of Mind,* Hutchinson & Company, Ltd., 1949.

- Searle, John, "Minds, Brains, and Programs," *Behavioral and Brain Sciences,* vol.3, Cambridge Univ. Press, 1980.

- Shakespeare, William, *Hamlet*, W. W. Norton & Company, 1963.

- Sheriff John K., *Charles Peirce's Guess at the Riddle, Grounds for Human Significance*, Indiana Univ. Press, 1994.

- Strawson, Galen, *Mental Reality*, The MIT Press, 1994.

- T'ang, Chün-i, "The Individual and the World in Chinese Methodology," *The Chinese Mind*, ed. by Charles A. Moore, University Press of Hawaii, 1977.

- Thayer, H. S., "Pragmatism,"*A Critical History of Western Philosophy*, Macmillan, 1964.

- Ware, James R., *The Saying of Chuang-Tzu a new Translation,* Confucius Publishing Co., 1959.

- Watts, Alan, *Tao: The Water Course Way*, Pelican Books, 1981.

- Wei, Tat, "Confucius and the I Ching, "*Chinese Philosophy,* Vol. 1, China Academy, 1974.

- Wittenborn, Allen, "Some Aspects of Mind and the Problem of Knowledge in Chu Hsi's Philosophy, "*Journal of Chinese Philosophy*, vol. 9, Dialogue Publishing Co., Honolulu, Hawaii, 1982.

Appendix: Korean Abstract

시공여인생 2
Space, Time and Life 2

이 저작물은 진정 나를 움직이도록 하는 작업이었다. 그 발상은 아버지 김충렬로 부터였다. 나의 아버지는 동양철학의 아버지였기도 했고, 지금도 그러하다. 43년 전 그는 자신의 첫 책을 중국어로 출판하였다; 『시공여인생(Space Time and Life)』. 그 때 그는 자신의 다섯 살인 아들, 나에게 그 책의 표지작업을 붓글씨로 하도록 했다. 『Space Time and Life』는 중국의 인식론과 형이상학을 주제로 다루었다. 지금 그 어린 아들이 『Space Time and Life 2』를 내놓게 되었는데, 이 책은 동·서 비교철학과 실용주의 철학을 인지과학이라는 테이블 위에서 총체적으로 논의한다. 이 새로운 장을 나는 "입체파 철학"이라고 부른다.

이 책은 인과적 결정론의 폐쇄성에 관한 책으로서, 한편에는 서양철학을 그리고 다른 한편에는 동양철학과 미국의 실용주의를 놓고 비교해 보는 책이다. 지금껏 많은 서양철학자들이 그들만의 잣대로 동양철학을 비판한 경우가 많았는데 이 책에서는 동양철학과 그와 유사한 실용주의를 기본으로 서양철학의 인식론적 태도를 비판할 것이다. 논의의 초점은 심리철학과 인지과학에 집중되어 시작될 것이고 마음에 대한 인과론적이고 결정론적인 접근이 불러오는 여러 문제점을 짚어 볼 것이다. 그 문제점들은 특히 인공지능에 대한 논의 과정에서 확연히 드러난다. 필자는 심리철학과 인지과학의 문제들이 그들의 방법론에 있는 것이 아니라 인식대상과 마음 사이의 인식의 형식에 있다고 보고, 이를 논증하기 위해 이 책의 중·후반부에서는 서양 고전철학의 인과론적 인식 체계와 이로 인한 현대 인지과학의 문제들을 들추어내고 동양철학과 실용주의 철학이 갖고 있는 상이한 인식론적 체계를 재평가해 봄으로써 돌파구를 제시하고자 한다.

서양철학에 있어서 인식의 형식은 '나'-인식자 vs '세계'-인식대상으로 이루어진 1 : 1 대응이다. 로크의 전통적 방식에 따르면 세계는 인식자의 마음 안에 비추어져 반영되며 (representationalism), 이 반영은 그것의 원인인 세상과 완전히 동일하지는 않다. 이것은 세상과 인식자에 대한 철저한 이분법이며, 학자들은 필연성의 확보를 위하여 인식 대상들 간의 선·후 원인(cause)들을 소급하여 올라간다. 원인 소급의 방법은 자연과학에서 많은 성과를 가져다주었으며 이로 인해 물리적 언어가 서양학문에 있어서 주요 방법론으로 자리를 굳혀갔다. 이 원인 소급의 방법과 물리적 방법론이 전적으로 잘못되었다는 것이 아니고 다만 이 방법이 철학에 있어서, 특히 심리철학에 있어서, 문제에 대한 가장 적절한 접근방식은 아니라는 것이다.

심리철학과 인지과학의 현주소는 현재의 형태로는 앞으로

더 나아갈 수 없는 한계에 와 있다고 보여 진다. 현재의 방법은 마치 색의 원리로 소리의 원리를 논한다거나 직선의 원리로 원의 원리를 논하는 것과 마찬가지이다, 서양철학의 이원론과 일원론 모두는 외부 물질세계를 결정론적인 법칙 하에서 인과적 방법으로 해석해 왔던 방식 그대로 마음의 문제를 다룬다. 그러면 우리는 왜 인과적 방법을 고수하여 왔는가? 필자는 그 원인이 서양철학이 수용하고 고수하고 있는 인식론적 자세와 형이상학적 체계에 있다고 본다, 그것은 우주자연에 대한 '교과서적 정답'을 얻으려 한 서양학문의 인식론적 자세 때문이다. 서양철학과 과학에서 우리는 확실성을 위해 인식자와 시·공을 통해 인식되는 외부대상을 구별하였고, 또 그 대상들이 선·후, 대·소를 따져 인과적 소급을 행하여 왔다. 마음에 대하여서도 심적 인과를 따진다. 여기서의 두 핵심 원리는 이분법과 인과적 소급이며 모든 개별대상과 사태들은 그것들이 현존하도록 한 선행원인들이 있어서 그 원인들 모두를 우리가 현재는 알 수 없더라도 그들은 지속적인 인과적 소급을 통하여 언젠가는 밝혀낼 수 있는 성질의 것이라는 믿음이다. 여기서 필자의 주장은 셋으로 요약될 수 있다. 첫째, 듀이(Dewey)와 동양철학의 인식태도에 따르자면 인식자는 인식대상, 즉 세계와 동떨어져 있는 것이 아니다. 이 세계의 어느 것도 순수한 독립체일 수 없다. 둘째, 인과적 소급은 우리를 변치 않는 정답으로 인도해 주지 않는다. 이 세상에는 변치 않는 고정적 개별자란 없다. 셋째, 인식자와 인식대상의 상호교섭에 의해서만 인식은 이루어진다.

프리고진이 엔트로피 법칙에서 말하듯 우주는 에너지의 평형과 비 평형 사이에서 지속적으로 변화한다. 한편에서는 에너지가 지속적으로 증가하여 카오스에 이르려 하고, 즉 지구 한편에서의 나비의 날갯짓이 지구 반대편에서의 폭풍과 같은 혼돈을 일으킬 수도 있고, 반대편에서는 산일구조 현상이 있어서 이에 대한 완충작용을 하여, 우주는 두 시스템의 상호작용으로 자기평정을 유지한다. 우주의 그 어떤 것도 이러한 '변화의 법칙'에서 제외되는 것은 없다. 우주는 생성, 소멸 사이클을 반복한다는 것이다. 듀이는 뉴턴의 작용과 반작용 원리를 이용하여 뉴턴적-고정적 우주관을 비판한다.

다음으로는 퍼스(Peirce)의 다원적 우주관이 있다. 둘 중 하나만을 정답이라고 할 수도 없고, 둘 다 함께 정답이라고 할 수도 없다. 이렇듯 우주와 자연에 대한 불변의 유일한 정답추구는 더 이상 옳은 자세가 아니다.

필자는 심리철학에서의 인지과학, 그리고 그중에서도 인공지능학도 우주자연에 대한 다른, 고양된 패러다임 위에서 새로운 자세로 두뇌현상 또는 마음에 대한 접근을 시도하여 보는 것이 바람직할지도 모른다고 생각한다. 우주자연현상이 불확실한 토대 위에서 이루어지고 있고 우리가 아는 한도 내에서 볼 때 정신현상이 자연현상의 정상에서 일어나는 현상이라 상정한다면, 정신현상의 불확실성을 추론해내는 것은 너무도 당연한 것이다. 불확정적 성격의 우주와 그에 대한 인식방법은 중국철학이나 실용주의 철학의 방법이 벌써부터 해왔던 내용들이므로 그 내용들을 연구해 봄직하다.

3장에서는 퍼스와 듀이의 마음에 대한 색다른 견해가 소개된다. 이들은 둘 다 다윈(Darwin)의 진화론 선상에서 일원론을 주장한다. 분명한 것은 퍼스와 듀이는 모두 과학적인 바탕에서 마음의 문제에 접근한다. 퍼스에게 있어서는 모든 사건이 복잡한 유기적 우주의 운행과정으로 인식된다. 퍼스는 마음이 이성, 의지, 감성이라는 구분(compartmentalization) 없이, 셋의 결합된 상태라고 주장한다. 듀이 또한 유기체적 우주관 속에서 창발적, 생물학적 일원론을 주장한다. 퍼스와 듀이는 이러한 일원론을 주장하지만 이는 정신현상을 물리적 현상으로 환원하여 소급하는 물리적 환원주의는 아니다. 이들의 일원론적 심리이론은 신비주의적이라는 분석철학의 비판을 받을 수 있겠으나, 듀이는 그의 생물학적 일원론(시·공 개념에 기초를 둠)에 대한 방어를 고전철학의 인식론과 형이상학에 대한 공격으로 대신한다. 퍼스와 듀이의 색다른 마음에 대한 견해는 그들만의 상이한 인식론과 형이상학적 체계에 기초를 두고 있다. 그러므로 이 책의 논의는 이러한 이유로 인식론과 형이상학을 다루지 않을 수 없었다.

퍼스와 듀이의 심리철학이 신비주의적이라는 비판에 대하여 듀이는 자신의 이론을 방어하는 방법으로 고전적 형이상학 체계를 비판하며 거기서 우리는 퍼스와 듀이의 심리철학의 이론이 나오게 된 그들의 형이상학적 배경을 엿볼 수 있다.

플라톤의 이데아론에서부터 내려오는 고전 형이상학의 형식은 이원론이다. 이는 데카르트에 와서 보다 정형화된 형식으로 확실성을 추구해 나가지만, 이원론 내의 존재들의 간격은 멀어져만 갔다. 그러나 과학의 발전으로 인해 이원론이든 아니든 서양철학은 더욱 더 물리적 언어로 고착되어 갔다. 그러므로 마음에 관하여도 물리적 언어로 해석을 하게 되므로 마음은 "해석불가능"으로 남는다.

듀이는 과학적 방법을 또 하나의 문제로 본다. 문제는 관찰대상을 대상자체로 보지 않고 원인추구의 방법으로 본다는 것이다. 퍼스의 주장은 이러한 관찰방법이 자연스러운 방법이 아니며, 이를 데카르트적 오류(Cartesian Mistake)라고 불렀다. 퍼스에게 있어서 의심이란 믿음같이 의지에 의한 것이다. 듀이와 퍼스는 원인추구의 방법으로 잘게 쪼개어진 사건의 조각들을 보다 확실하다고 보는 종적인 인식구조를 거부한다.

듀이에 따르면, 세계의 모든 것들은 횡적인 관계에서 서로 영향을 주고받는 유기체적 형식 내에 있고 그 어느 것도 부동적이지 않아서 마치 고정화되어 있는 듯한 개체들을 보다 나은 확실성을 위하여 인과적 분해를 시도하는 방법(관람자 이론, spectator theory)이 잘못되었다는 것이다. 그러므로 퍼스와 듀이는 이원론에 입각한 몸과 마음의 구분에 반대하고, 단지 마음이란 물리적인 현상의 최상위 단계에서 특이하게 일어나는, 우리가 물리적인 방법으로만은 해석할 수 없는 현상으로만 보는 것이다. 우주는 너무도 크고 방대하며, 그 구성체들은 항상 그리고 지속적으로 변화하며, 서로 간에 상호작용을 해 나아가고 있으므로, 우리가 알 수 있는 것이란 항상 우주의 작은 일부의 내용일 뿐이라고, 우리의 인식의 한계를 수용하는 것이 퍼스와 듀이의 우주관이다.

여기서 우리가 중국철학으로 눈을 돌려볼 때, 애초부터 전체론적(holistic) 일원론에서 시작하여 초 물리적 불확정성 위에서 철학의 체계를 성립하여온 그들의 인식론과 형이상학을 연구해봄직 하다고 생각된다. 우선 4장에서는 중국철학 내의 '마음'에 대한 이론에서 시작하여 형이상학으로 논의의 초점을 옮겨갔으며, 5장에서는 이를 퍼스와 듀이의 체계와 비교해 보았다,

서양의 인지과학자들의 눈에는 중국철학이 비합리적이며 신비론적으로 보이겠지만, 그 근본인 상이함은 서양철학의 인과적 인식형태와 결정론적인 세계관에 대비되는 중국철학의 유기체적 세계관에서 비롯된다. 이러한 이유로 4장의 논의는 결국 중국철학의 인식론과 형이상학적 체계로 그 방향을 몰아갔다.

공자가 말하길 성상근, 습상원(性相近, 習相遠)이라 했다. 이는 후천적 생명정신이 단계적으로 층차적 발전을 한다고 보았기 때문이다. 첫째로 물질의 정(精)을 정순(精純)이라고 한다. 사람이 어떤 음식을 섭취하느냐에 따라 정(精)의 활력이 달라진다는 것이다. 이는 유물론적 견해가 아닐 수 없다. 두 번째는 생명의 정(精)인데 이를 정기(精氣)라고 한다. 물질 섭

취를 바탕으로 생겨난 기력(氣力)·활력(活力)을 생명의 의식 단계로 상승시키는 일이다. 세 번째는 심지(心知)의 정인데 이를 정신(精神)이라고 한다. 어떤 일을 집중 단련 공부하면 마치 지력에 활연관통(豁然貫通)하는 예지력이 생기는 것처럼 신명력이 생겨난다는 것이다. 이렇듯 정신에 대한 단계적 발전-승화 이론은 유물론과 유심론이 복합되어 있으며 정신을 단계적으로 구분하여 본 방법론은 앞에서 논의한 듀이의 생물학적 일원론과 유사한 구조이다.

몸과 마음의 반-이원론적인 존재론적 관계는 주희(朱熹) 이후 중국철학의 이(理)·기(氣)론의 방법론적 논의구성을 살펴보면 이해에 도움이 된다. Wen-Shan Huang(黃文山)이 주희의 이·기론을 해석하기를 천지간에 리(理)도 있고 기(氣)도 있다. 리는 형이상(形而上)의 노(道)요 생물의 근본이며, 기는 형이하(形而下)의 기(器)요 생물의 구상(具象)이라 하였다. 그러므로 만물이 생(生)한다고 하는 것은 반드시 이 리를 품수(稟受 innate)한 뒤라야 성신(性神)을 발할 수 있고, 반드시 기를 구유(具有)한 뒤라야 형체를 갖출 수 있다. 이·기에 관해서 중국철학 내에서도 여러 상이한 이론들이 있다. 한대(漢代)의 주기론(主氣論)에서는 태극(太極)을 원기(元氣), 즉 음양(陰陽)이 아직 갈라지지 않은 혼일(混一)의 기요 리는 기의 변화법칙과 만유(萬有)의 질서로서 기의 속성으로 보았고, 주희와 정이(程頤)는 기는 리의 사역(使役)이 되는 위치에 두어보고, 종적(縱的)인 선후를 따질 때에는 리가 기에 대하여 상위개념이라고

Wen-Shan Huang은 보았다. 그러나 한대의 이·기 개념이나 주희의 이·기론 모두 만물이 생성하는 과정에서 리 없는 기가 있을 수 없고 기 없는 리가 존재할 수 없다고 하였다.

서양의 기준으로 볼 때 비합리적이고 비과학적이라고 보일 수밖에 없는 중국철학내의 여러 심·신 이론들은 어떻게 이러한 서양철학의 논박을 피할 수 있을 것인가? 중국철학 내에도 천지만물의 생성의 시단(始端)을 소급해 가려는 시도가 있다. 만물은 음(陰)·양(陽)으로 이루어져 있고 음양은 태극(Supreme Ultimate)에서 왔다. 일반적으로 유가(儒家)에서는 태극을 만물 생성의 최상위 개념으로 보고 소급의 선을 긋는다.

5장에서는 퍼스의 Tychism과 Syhechism이라는 용어로 부른 퍼스의 유기체적 우주론을 소개하고 이를 노자(老子)의 '도'사상과 비교해 볼 것이다. 퍼스는 세상의 양면성을 이야기한다. 우리가 알 수 없는 세상의 진정한 내용을 Tychism이라 부르고, 알 수 있는 내용을 Synechism이라 부른다. Tychism(원인 없는 사건)은 그 진정한 원인이 없다는 것은 아니고 순수하게 우연한 원인에 의한 사건이기 때문에 그 원인의 진위를 규명할 수 없으며, 이것이 우주의 참모습이라 말한다. 그렇다면 우리는 어떻게 세상에 대한 지식을 가질 수 있는가? 우연히 일어나는 사건들 중 반복해서 일어나는 사건들에 대하여는 우리가 인위적으로 규율성을 부여하여 지식으로 삼는데 이러한 사건들의 내용을 퍼스는 Synechism이라 부르며 이를 자연과학의 대상으로 본다. 퍼스는 우주가 지속적으로 진화해 간다고 보고 우리의 지식도 마찬가지로 지속적으로 쌓여가며 진화해 간다고 말한다.

퍼스는 서양의 자연과학이 선행원인을 규명하여 그것을 우주에 대한 교과서적 정답으로 여기는 것에 반대한다. 퍼스의 이러한 우주관은 노자의 '도'사상과 비교될 수 있다. Man-jan Cheng의 해석에 의하면 노자가 제1장에서 말하길 도를 도라 말할 수 있다면 그 도는 변화하는 현상 하에 있는 도이고 전체의 일부인 도이지 모두를 포괄하고 영원히 변화를 지속하는 전체의 모습, 즉 시(時)·공(空)을 초월해서 스스로 그렇게 있는 도는 아니라고 한다(道可道 非常道). 앞의 도는 인식 가능한 도이고 따라서 말할 수 있는 것이지만 뒤의 도는 규명하기 어려운 전체 포괄의 도이다. 노자는 진정한 도의 개념을 후자의 도에 두었다. 퍼스가 근본적으로 세계를 알 수 있는 세계(Synechism)와 알 수 없는 세계(Tychism)로 구분한 이원론직 우주관에서 형이상학적 체계를 구축하였다면 노자의 도와 상도(常道) 사이에는 확연한 경계의 선이 없이 다만 감관을 통한 인식의 방법과 한계가 다르다는 것이므로 이원론적 시발이 아니라는 점에서 퍼스의 체계와 차이가 있다. 그러나 인식론적 차원에서 본다면 세상에 대한 일반적 인식이 양분된 점에서, 도를 서양적 개념으로 '세계원리'라고 할 때 노자의 '도'개념 중 '알 수 있는 도(道)'와 '규명하기 어려운 도(道)'는 평행선상에서 퍼스의 Syhechism 과 Tychism과 연결지을 수 있다.

듀이는 서양의 이분법적 인식형태를 부정하고 인식자와 인식대상 간의 연속적인 상호교섭에 의한 인식형태를 주장한다. 듀이는 인식의 주체이건 대상이건 간에 이 세상에는 완전히 독립적이고 고정적인 개별자가 있을 수 없다고 주장한다. 그에 의하면 인식주체인 우리는 인식대상인 세상에 부착되어 있어서 순수한 개별자나 개별자에 대한 순수 개별적 인식은 없다는 것이다. 이는 훗날 로티(Rorty)의 신 실용주의에서 반-반영주의 와 반-정초주의라는 이름으로 그 명맥을 이어 가게 된다.

James R. Ware의 장자에 대한 번역에 의하면 장자는 세상을 육합지내(六合之內)와 육합지외(六合之外)로 나누어 보고 육합지외를 괄호 안에 넣어 두고 일반 인식 외의 문제로 놓아둔다. James R. Ware의 해석에 의하면 장자(莊子)가 말하길 도통위일(道通爲一)이라 했다. '나'의 본성의 광명지혜(光明知慧)를 통해서 도를 각득(覺得)하면 결국은 '나'와 도가 둘이 아니고 하나라는 것을 깨닫는다는 것이다. 중국철학에 있어서 분별지(分別智), 즉 나와 대상을 둘로 갈라놓은 전제에서 차별, 분별을 추구해 가는 지식은 정확성을 확보할 수 있으나 이는 인간과 인간, 인간과 자연 등을 갈라놓아 역기능의 부작용이 발생한다고 보았다.

도가(道家)의 인식론은 인식하는 자와 인식대상을 개별적 '둘'에서 총체적 '하나'로 합치는 과정을 추구한다. 불가의 기본적 인식체계에서도 인식의 초기 단계에서는 인식하는 자와 인식되는 세계가 구별되어 있으나 인식의 과정에서 둘의 경계가 사라져서 결국 '하나'가 된다고 말한다. 듀이의 인식론과 장자를 중심으로 한 중국의 인식론 체계는, 인식자와 인식대상의 구별을 부정하고 상호교섭 내지는 인식론적 일원론을 주장한다. 그러므로 듀이와 장자의 인식론적 기본자세를 서양적 개념으로 이름 짓는다면 '인식론적 일원론'이라 부를 수 있을 것이다. 이를 Wing-Tsit Chan(陳榮捷)은 'oneness'라 부르고, Thomé H. Fang(方東美)은 이를 '포괄적 조화(comprehensive harmony)'라고 부른다. 이러한 인식론적 체계는 서양 인과론의 근간이 되는 인식자와 인식대상에 대한 이분법과 확연히 대비된다.

이 책에서 논의된 내용은 심리철학의 제 문제가 인과적 폐쇄성과 인식과정의 이분법적 접근에서 비롯되었다는 것이다. 이 책의 목차와 구성을 얼핏 보기에는 동·서양철학의 여러 분야와 분과들이 두서없이 나열되어 비교된 듯 보일 수도 있을 것이다. 그러나 필자는 서양철학의 인과적 결정론의 체계를 재평가하기 위하여 심리철학과 인지과학을 논의의 테이블 위에 올려놓아 논의의 화두로 삼았으며 이를 논하는 과정에서 드러나는 인과론의 폐쇄성의 문제점들을 들추어냄에 있어서 그 근본 문제를 인식론과 형이상학의 차원의 문제로 끌어올려 서양철학의 영역 밖의 사고체계를 소개하고 비교 논의하는 목적으로 중국철학과 서양철학이면서도 그 근본체계가 중국철학과 유사한 퍼스와 듀이의 인식체계를 논의하였다.

이것은 분과들 간의 크로스오버가 갖은 큰 가치중 하나이다. 서양의 자연과학과 결정론의 토대에서 신비론에 대한 작은 공간을 허용한다면, 서양의 심리철학 또는 서양철학자체는 그들의 체계외적인 중국철학과 실용주의 철학 같은 비주류이론들을 한번 검토하여 보는 방법을 통해 새로운 방향도 고려해봄직도 하지 않을까 생각된다. 필자의 주장은 비주류이론들이 옳다는 것이 아니다. 본문에서 주장된 바와 같이 “정답은 없다.” 그러나 현 패러다임의 통념과 경계선을 허물고 비주류적 방법들을 포괄적으로 담은 연구는 새롭고 보다 나은 방향의 제시를 이룰 수 있으리라 생각한다.

Kim, Jeong-il Ph.D.

[Current Status]

Director of JungCheon Philosophy Foundation, Seoul Korea

[Academic background]

B.S.(Philosophy) University of Kansas at Lawrence, U.S.A

M.S.(Philosophy) California State University at Los Angeles, U.S.A

Ph.D.(Philosophy) Dongguk University at Seoul Korea

[Lecturer]

Department of Philosophy, Dongguk University, Korea

Department of Philosophy, Kangwon University, Korea

Department of Philosophy, Hankuk University of Foreign Studies, Korea

Visiting Professor, Shaanxi Normal University, China

[Other Professional Career]

Professional Member of Bioethics Committee, Korea University

[Publication / Articles]

Kim, Jeong-Il, Don Quixote Philosophy, Edambooks, Seoul, 2010.

Kim, Jeong-Il, "Peirce's Unique System of Pragmatism," World Congress of Philosophers, Seoul Korea, 2008. [e-book]

Kim, Jeong-Il, "A Comparative Study on Yin/Yang Principle and Modern Reproduction Technology," Eastern Philosophy, vol. 25, 2006.

Kim, Jeong-Il, "Dewey's and Chuang Tzu's epistemology of 'oneness',"

Chinese Philosophy, vol. 12, 2004.

Kim, Jeong-Il, "Dewey's biological account on mind," Philosophcal Thought, vol. 22, 2004.

Kim, Jeong-Il, "Peirce's cosmology compared with Lao Tzu's concept of 'Tao'," Saehan Association of Philosophy, vol. 37, 2004.

[Address]

Email: philomentor@naver.com

Homepage: www.jungcheon.net